Critical Thinking

How to Make Smarter Decisions, Conquer Logical Fallacies

(A Fundamental Guide to Effective Decision Making, Deep Analysis)

Harold Colon

Published By **Darby Connor**

Harold Colon

All Rights Reserved

Critical Thinking: How to Make Smarter Decisions, Conquer Logical Fallacies (A Fundamental Guide to Effective Decision Making, Deep Analysis)

ISBN 978-1-7750277-7-5

No part of this guidebook shall be reproduced in any form without permission in writing from the publisher except in the case of brief quotations embodied in critical articles or reviews.

Legal & Disclaimer

The information contained in this book is not designed to replace or take the place of any form of medicine or professional medical advice. The information in this book has been provided for educational & entertainment purposes only.

The information contained in this book has been compiled from sources deemed reliable, and it is accurate to the best of the Author's knowledge; however, the Author cannot guarantee its accuracy and validity and cannot be held liable for any errors or omissions. Changes are periodically made to this book. You must consult your doctor or get professional medical advice before using any of the suggested remedies, techniques, or information in this book.

Upon using the information contained in this book, you agree to hold harmless the Author from and against any damages, costs, and expenses, including any legal fees potentially resulting from the application of any of the information provided by this guide. This disclaimer applies to any damages or injury caused by the use and application, whether directly or indirectly, of any advice or information presented, whether for breach of contract, tort, negligence, personal injury, criminal intent, or under any other cause of action.

You agree to accept all risks of using the information presented inside this book. You need to consult a professional medical practitioner in order to ensure you are both able and healthy enough to participate in this program.

Table Of Contents

Chapter 1: Critical Thinking Defining 1

Chapter 2: The Components Of Critical Thinking 11

Chapter 3: Developing A Critical Mindset 28

Chapter 4: Effective Communication And Critical Thinking 44

Chapter 5: Applying Critical Thinking In Different Academic Disciplines 61

Chapter 6: Strategies For Problem-Solving And Decision Making 77

Chapter 7: Overcoming Challenges In Critical Thinking 93

Chapter 8: Critical Thinking 109

Chapter 9: Developing Intellectual Humility 121

Chapter 10: Analyzing Arguments And Evidence 131

Chapter 11: Decision Making And Uncertainty 139

Chapter 12: Critical Thinking In Media And Information Literacy 150

Chapter 13: Decoding Complexity In Politics 161

Chapter 14: The Concept Of Critical Thinking 169

Chapter 15: Understanding Information Overload 177

Chapter 16: The Fundamentals Of Critical Thinking 180

Chapter 1: Critical Thinking Defining

In the current information-driven and fast-paced society, skills of critical thinking have become more essential than they ever were. As students, we receive an abundance of data that comes from a variety of sources. Therefore, it's essential to know how to sift through the plethora of information, consider the implications and make educated choices. The subchapter titled "Defining Critical Thinking," is designed to lay the groundwork to master the process of critical thinking. It will also equip you with essential techniques to succeed in your studies.

Then, what do you mean by critical thinking? Simply put it is the capacity to examine and assess the arguments, information or ideas with a clear and rational way. This goes beyond simply believing in what you read and encourages you to think critically, examine and challenge your assumptions. The key to critical thinking is being open looking at different viewpoints, using reasoning in order to come up with well-thought-out conclusions.

The development of critical thinking abilities is essential to successful academic performance. This allows you to interact in the course content in a deeper way, pose meaningful questions, and connect across different ideas. As you develop your critical-thinking capabilities, you will are able to be an active student in your own learning instead of just a passive consumer of knowledge.

Through this book in which we explore various areas of critical thinking which includes how to recognize the biases of our thinking, assess evidence, and formulate compelling arguments. In this book, we will discuss the significance of logic as well as problem-solving and decisions. Learn ways to increase the analytical abilities of your students like thinking about, brainstorming, and reviewing sources to determine their trustworthiness and authenticity.

Furthermore, this chapter will also introduce you to fundamental characteristics of a critically thinker. The focus will be on the significance of humility in the mind, intellectual intelligence, and curiosity. Learn the best ways to address complex questions with a wide-ranging mind. constantly seeking out different perspectives as well as critically evaluate your assumptions and prejudices.

If you can master the skill of critical thinking you'll not only be able to achieve academic excellence, but you will also acquire capabilities that are sought-after within the workplace. Employers look for individuals who be able to think through problems, make decisions and take informed decision-making. The ability to think critically is a long-lasting capability that is beneficial throughout your day-to-day life.

Get ready to go into a journey that will transform your learning and academic achievement. Let's explore the realm of critical thinking and arm our minds with the right tools to master the challenges of our information-driven world.

The Importance of Critical Thinking in Academic Success

The Importance of Critical Thinking in Academic Success

In our fast-paced, information-driven society, skills in critical thinking have become more essential more than ever to achieve high academic achievement. Students are constantly bombarded with an overwhelming quantity of data from a variety of sources. It is therefore essential to build and strengthen the ability to think critically. Critical thinking is an ability that allows us to think critically as well as evaluate the information in a way that allows our to take informed choices and resolve complex challenges.

One of the major reasons why critical thinking is crucial to academic achievement is its capacity to improve our knowledge of what we are exposed to. When we apply critical thinking techniques will allow us to dig more deeply into the subject to challenge assumptions, as well as look at different viewpoints. This helps us understand the subject better however it allows us to gain a deeper and complete understanding of the subject that we are dealing with.

Furthermore, critical thinking allows individuals to judge the validity and credibility of data we find. Due to the increasing prevalence of false news and misleading information and misinformation, knowing how to distinguish reliable sources from those that aren't is vital. Critical thinking helps us determine the truthfulness of statements as well as identify the source of bias and differentiate between facts and opinions. Through developing our critical thinking capabilities, we are able to become knowledgeable consumers of information which can be a great resource in any academic environment.

Critical thinking also enhances thinking skills that are analytical and problem solving. With our critical thinking skills, we can learn to dissect complex questions into more accessible pieces that allow us to spot patterns, connections and possible solutions. This is particularly useful for those fields that demand logic and reasoning like sciences, math, and engineering. As we develop our critical thinking capabilities, we can become better at tackling complex challenges, coming up with new solutions, and communicate our thinking process.

Additionally, critical thinking encourages the development of autonomous and independent learning. Through challenging the assumptions of our teachers and challenging their knowledge, we build a curiosity about the world and take part within our own learning. The process of critical thinking allows learners to explore the subject matter in an active manner, look for different perspectives, and formulate our own views. It not only results in an enriching experience in learning but also fosters a lifetime enthusiasm for studying.

Critical thinking is a crucial aspect in academic achievement cannot be overemphasized. It allows us to go more deeply into a subject to assess the reliability of the information we are given, increase our skills in problem solving, and promote the ability to learn independently. When they master the skills of critical thinking students are able to navigate the maze of the academic world with confidence which will allow them to succeed at their academics and even beyond.

The Benefits of Developing Critical Thinking Skills

In our fast-paced and constantly changing environment, developing critical thinking abilities is crucial for those trying to be successful in their academic pursuits. Critical thinking refers to the capacity to evaluate, analyze and comprehend data in a rational and systematic manner. It's a technique that is more than memorization. It allows students to think for themselves to question the assumptions of others and formulate well-thought-out arguments. The subchapter below will examine the various benefits that are associated from developing skills in critical thinking and provide students with an understanding of the reasons what it takes to be a critical component of academic achievement.

Most importantly, the ability to think critically allows learners to become better problem-solvers. When faced with challenges using an open mind, they are able to determine what is causing the issue, analyze various perspectives and suggest new solutions. This ability allows them to handle difficult academic assignments, like groups or research papers efficiently and with confidence.

Additionally, developing critical-thinking abilities improves the ability of students to assess and analyse the information. In a world of constant the influx of information, students must to know how to distinguish between credible sources and misleading sources of information. Critical thinking provides them with tools for assessing the accuracy, reliability as well as the biases of different sources. This allows them to make informed choices and avoid being a victim of inaccurate information.

Critical thinking abilities stimulate creativity and encourage innovation. In a way, by stimulating students to think outside the boundaries, think critically about their the assumptions they make and to explore different viewpoints, critical thinking stimulates the students' imagination and allows them to come up with original concepts. The ability to think in a creative manner is a must in the academic setting, where students often have to provide fresh perspectives and innovative research.

Furthermore that, the skills of critical thinking contribute in delivering a clear message. students who have the ability to critically analyze and assess information can better articulate their opinions and thoughts effectively. They are able to formulate well-thought-out arguments, justify their opinions with proof, and engage with others in meaningful debates. The ability to communicate effectively is not solely essential for academic achievement, but are also essential to improve personal and professional growth.

Additionally, developing the ability to think critically is a key ingredient in continuous learning. Through cultivating a sense of curiosity and doubt the students are active learners, seeking more knowledge outside of the classroom. They are self-directed learners that seek out different ideas, challenge the assumptions of their parents, and continually expand their possibilities.

Chapter 2: The Components Of Critical Thinking

Analyzing Information

Today, in the age of information the ability to examine and assess the huge variety of information available is an essential skill to ensure academic achievement. In this section we'll explore how to analyze the information available and give you concrete strategies for improving your ability to critically think.

One of the initial steps in the process of analyzing data is gathering relevant information from trusted sources. Due to the increasing amount of information available on the web, it's vital to examine the authenticity and reliability of the sources you rely on. This article will explore methods like cross-referencing, fact-checking and checking the skills of the author to be sure the data you trust is reliable and of top quality.

After you've gathered all the required details, now it's time to look at the information. This is the process of breaking down large concepts and ideas into easily digestible pieces. The course will teach you different methods of analysis for example, identifying important arguments, looking at evidence as well as spotting logic-based fallacies. As you develop these skills it will become easier to analyze arguments, comprehend the assumptions behind them, and identify the flaws and inconsistencies.

In addition, we'll dive into the necessity of active reading and involvement with texts. Just skimming over the material isn't enough. Instead we'll guide readers through the process of reading through asking questions, creating connections, and then taking notes. These methods will allow you to comprehend the primary ideas and identify evidence to support them, and determine the general quality of the material.

To increase your understanding and improve your analytical abilities We will also look at ways of comparing and contrast different sources of information. When you compare multiple perspectives it will allow you to recognize biases, analyze the strengths and weaknesses of each as well as develop a balanced view of a particular topic. This is particularly useful in the academic setting as the ability to take a different perspective is extremely sought-after.

We will also examine the ethical consequences for analyzing information. Since information can be altered and altered for a variety of purposes and purposes, it's important to evaluate ethics of data we come across. The course will examine concepts including media literacy propaganda, and the significance to consider different perspectives.

When you master the art of analysing data, you'll improve your ability to think critically as well as become an educated and knowledgeable scholar. When you're conducting research, writing essays or taking part in discussions with your class The ability to think about data critically can make you stand out in the field of academic success. Thus, get into this section and arm yourself with the necessary tools to navigate through the maze of data with ease and accuracy.

Evaluating Arguments

Students among the most essential abilities we have to acquire can be critical thought. Today's world is extremely fast-paced the ability to analyze arguments in a way that is effective is crucial to the success of your academic career. In this chapter we'll explore how to evaluate arguments. We will provide strategies and tools to develop into a skilled critical thinker.

Before we begin, let's look at the meaning of an argument. A formal argument is a collection of arguments, wherein some or all of the assumptions are put forward to back up an argument. Knowing the form of an argument can be vital because it allows us to assess the legitimacy of the argument that is presented. The next step is to discover assumptions, conclusions, as well as their logical relationships.

If we are evaluating arguments, it is important to have to differentiate between weak and strong arguments. A strong argument occurs that has sufficient evidence to justify the argument, whereas an argument that is weak lacks evidence or has logical flaws. This article examines common errors and the best ways to recognize and avoid them, thus allowing you to build a critical mind for flawed reasoning.

A crucial aspect to consider when reviewing arguments is to evaluate the reliability and credibility of the source. It is essential to take into consideration the knowledge and beliefs of the author to evaluate whether their assertions are true. There will be strategies to checking sources such as checking credentials, cross-referencing data as well as identifying biases.

We will also look at the significance of evidence when it comes to evaluating arguments. Knowing the distinction between evidence based on anecdotes and actual evidence, and understanding the significance of statistical information, will allow the ability to make informed decisions. In addition, we will consider the necessity of taking into consideration possible counterarguments as well as addressing challenges to your argument.

Finally, we'll concentrate on enhancing your critical thinking abilities through reflection and practice. Studying case studies, as well as taking part in discussions with others improve your capacity to critically evaluate arguments. We'll provide actual exercises and instances to sharpen your thinking abilities and use them in various subjects in the academic world.

If you can master the art of critically evaluating arguments, you'll increase your academic performance, but develop a better discerning shopper of knowledge. Thinking about your thoughts is an ability which will benefit you throughout your entire academic career. Let's begin this thrilling journey together, to unlock the power of critical thinking to achieve academic achievement!

Problem-Solving Techniques

In the world of academics critical thinking plays crucial roles in academic performance. Students, it's vital to learn effective problem-solving methods that can help us to conquer obstacles and succeed in the classroom. This chapter aims at providing the reader with helpful information and methods to increase your thinking abilities that will enable you to solve difficult academic issues efficiently and with confidence.

The most important methods of problem solving is the use of analysis. This is the process of breaking down complicated issues into smaller, easily manageable parts. When you take the time to examine each component it will give you an comprehension of the issue in general and pinpoint possibilities for solutions. This method of analysis helps you approach issues in a systematic manner, making sure that none of the important details are left unnoticed.

Additionally, this chapter introduces the idea of brainstorming. Brainstorming is a great method to generate a variety of possible solutions and concepts. Through encouraging creativity and free-thinking it allows one to think about different options and perspectives. This chapter provides guidelines for conducting effective brainstorming sessions. It also provides suggestions to foster a healthy and productive environment.

In addition, this chapter stresses the importance of a critical evaluation when it comes to problem solving. It introduces strategies like SWOT analysis (Strengths weaknesses, Strengths Opportunities, threats) as well as cost-benefit analysis which aids in determining the potential outcomes and viability of various options. Through analyzing the advantages and disadvantages of each option and making informed choices that will lead to the best result.

A different important technique for problem solving that is covered in this chapter is the idea of iteration. Iteration is the process of testing and refining strategies. When you seek feedback, studying outcomes, and making the necessary changes, you will increase your effectiveness in problem solving methods. This chapter offers practical suggestions about how you can incorporate the process of iteration in your approach to problem solving.

The subchapter also highlights the importance of perseverance and perseverance in tackling problems. It is true that academic problems can be challenging and require multiple attempts to come up with a feasible solution. With a positive outlook and accepting challenges as an opportunity to develop, you'll be able beat obstacles and attain the academic excellence you desire.

The section on problem-solving strategies offers students useful strategies for enhancing the ability of their brains to think critically. Through integrating an analytical approach, brainstorming techniques and critical evaluation, as well as the process of iteration and perseverance in their process of problem solving Students can conquer difficulties in academics and succeed at their academics. These methods are vital tools to help students achieve academic success with the help of their the ability to think critically.

Decision Making

:

On our way to academic success, one of the skills which is of great importance is making decisions. Students are always faced with decisions which can affect our learning experiences and affect the direction of our lives. Making the right decisions making is a crucial aspect of thinking critically, which allows individuals to make well-informed decisions and make sense of the complexity of university. In this chapter, we look at the principles and methods of successful decision-making, helping students to be a proficient and effective decision maker.

1. The Importance of Decision Making:

Each day, students face numerous choices that range from choosing a course and choosing the best study methods. The importance of decisions making is essential, because it affects the direction that we choose to take as well as the results that we can achieve. If we can improve our decision-making abilities will help us improve our academic achievement, decrease anxiety, and make the most of our academic possibilities.

2. The Decision-Making Process:

For effective decision-making to make effective decisions, we require a well-organized strategy. In this section, we will guide the steps of a procedure for making decisions that involves the identification, analysis, and evaluation as well as execution. In this section, we'll go over each step and explore methods like the process of brainstorming, SWOT analysis and decision matrixes for thorough decisions.

3. Decision-Making Biases and Pitfalls:

We have a tendency to make mistakes as well as cognitive shortcuts which can make it difficult to make decisions. Being aware of and combating the effects of these biases is essential to making logical and rational choices. In this section, we will discuss some of the common biases like anchoring bias, confirmation bias and confirmation bias. We will provide ways to counter them, while ensuring that your choices are informed by accurate data as well as sound reasoning.

4. Ethical Decision Making:

Ethics plays a crucial role in the process of making decisions, especially when it comes to academics. In this section, we will highlight the significance of considering ethical issues and examine ethical models for decision making. Incorporating ethical concepts in your decision-making process you'll not just take decisions that are in line to your beliefs, but help create a more ethical and compassionate community of academics.

5. Decision Making in Group Settings:

Collaboration in decision-making is an essential element of academic achievement. When we are students, we frequently are working as groups or taking part in group assignments. This guide will arm students with techniques to guide the group's decision-making process, promote an effective dialogue, establish consensus, and solve conflicts. Through harnessing the collective intellect of your colleagues and making educated decisions that are beneficial to all members of the group.

The ability to make decisions is a crucial ability for those who want to achieve success in their studies. If you can understand the process of decision making by recognizing the biases that affect you, applying ethics and mastering group decision-making, you'll be a skilled decision-maker and able to make sound decisions that will shape your academic experience. Keep in mind that choosing a course of action is not only focused on the results but concerning the entire process making sure that your decisions are informed by the critical and reflective reasoning.Creativity and ingenuity

Creativity and Innovation: Unleashing the Power of Critical Thinking

:

Today's fast-changing world Critical thinking abilities have been deemed essential to academic performance. This chapter explores the ever-changing interaction between innovation, creativity as well as critical thinking. Through understanding and mastering these concepts, students are able to increase their ability to critically think, tackle issues, and succeed in their academic endeavors.

Exploring Creativity:

The fuel for creativity is what sparks the flame of creativity. It's a process that involves creating original concepts, distinctive ideas, and innovative ideas. When it comes to academics creative thinking goes far over the boundaries of the arts, and is applicable to every discipline. This allows students to take their courses with new ideas, challenge the established wisdom, and uncover the possibilities that are new.

Fostering a Creative Mindset:

To foster their creativity, they need to embrace a positive attitude. It involves opening themselves to new perspectives while also letting go of judgement as well as exploring different perspectives. Through embracing a growth-oriented perspective, students will be able to transcend the self-imposed limits, accept the uncertainty and unleash their potential for creativity. Participating in tasks like thinking about, brainstorming as well as free writing may help stimulate creativity.

The Role of Innovation:

Innovation is the implementation of ideas that are creative that result in tangible benefits. It is about exploring, taking risks in the pursuit of solutions to tackle real-world issues. By embracing innovation, students are able to improve their educational experience, conduct cutting-edge research and make important contributions to their field of research.

The Intersection of Critical Thinking, Creativity, and Innovation:

Critical thinking acts as the mainstay between innovation and creativity. It is the process of analyzing, evaluating and synthesising information in order for making informed choices. When you incorporate critical thinking into the process of creativity Students can evaluate whether or not they are able to implement their creative ideas. They can ensure that their creative ideas are well-thought-out, based on evidence and able to withstand examination.

Developing Creative and Innovative Thinking Skills:

To foster creative and imaginative thinking, students may use a range of techniques. They can use lateral thinking whereby problems are approached in a new way, and reframing, in which you look at problems through different perspectives. Design activities for thinking, as well as experiences with different perspectives may help develop these abilities.

Creativity and ingenuity are crucial elements of critical thinking to ensure academic achievement. If you embrace a visionary approach, students will be able to tap their potential to the fullest, develop new ideas and tackle problems with new perspectives. Incorporating critical thinking into the process of creativity ensures that creative solutions are sound and effective.

Chapter 3: Developing A Critical Mindset

Recognizing Biases and Assumptions

For academic success, among the most essential skills you can learn is the ability to think critically. Thinking criticalally allows students to think critically, analyze the information they are presented with, make judgments about arguments and make educated decisions. The art of critical thinking is more than logic and problem-solving. It involves recognizing biases and confronting them and preconceived notions.

Assumptions and biases are imbedded in our mental patterns, and often influence our behavior and thoughts even without conscious thought. These can be a result of our the experiences of our own lives, influences from culture and social norms. Understanding these assumptions and biases are crucial as they may impair our judgement, limit our ability to comprehend, and ultimately cause a faulty understanding.

A common bias is the confirmation bias. This is the tendency of us to look for information which confirms our assumptions and dismiss or ignore any evidence that contradicts these beliefs. The bias may prevent students from exploring alternative perspectives and hamper their ability consider their ideas about their thinking. If they are aware of this bias students will be able to seek various perspectives and sources of evidence for a broad knowledge of any topic.

Another potential bias worth being aware of is the bias to availability which is when we depend heavily on data that is easily accessible and we ignore other data that is relevant. This could lead to poor reasoning or inconclusive evaluations. When they are aware of this bias students should make an attempt to collect comprehensive and accurate information prior to drawing or taking decisions.

Assumptions on contrary, are opinions or beliefs that are regarded as normal without a sufficient basis or evidence. They may be founded on generalizations, stereotypes or a lack of information. Be aware of assumptions as they can result in faulty reasoning, and hinder students from pursuing alternative options. Through challenging their assumptions and looking for arguments to refute or support their validity, students will improve their ability to think critically and come to more precise conclusions.

To be able to identify biases, assumptions and prejudices Students should develop self-awareness, and be willing to question the way they think. They need to be open critique and be willing to look at other views. Engaging in constructive discussion and debating with friends could help them recognize the biases and assumptions that are present in their arguments, and help them develop ability to think critically.

Understanding implicit biases and beliefs is a crucial aspect of learning the art that is critical thinking. When we are conscious of our own biases and challenging assumptions Students can increase their ability to be able to think critically and evaluate data objectively and make informed decisions. The development of this ability is essential to succeed in school and beyond as it allows students to tackle difficult issues engaging in thoughtful conversations, and be a part of the world as educated and responsible people.

Overcoming Cognitive Biases

To achieve academic excellence, developing analytical skills is essential. One of the biggest obstacles that can hinder the ability of our brains to think critically is existence in our brains cognitive biases. They are mental tricks that brains employ to make it easier for us to process complex information. Although they can be beneficial in certain circumstances, they could hinder our ability to consider our thoughts critically and objectively.

The ability to recognize and overcome cognitive biases is a crucial stage in understanding the process in critical thinking.

In understanding these biases, and learning techniques to reduce the effects of them, students will improve their abilities to analyze the information in a precise manner and take informed choices.

The most common cognitive bias we face is the confirmation bias. It is the tendency of us to look for and evaluate data that supports our current views or beliefs. The bias may prevent our minds from considering different perspectives or looking at evidence that contradicts the assumptions we have. In order to overcome the confirmation bias, students need to actively look for different perspectives, participate with open-minded debates and analyze data from diverse sources.

Another common skepticism can be the availability heuristic which is where we base our decisions on the immediately-remembered examples that pop into our minds when making decisions or taking decisions. The bias could lead to underestimating the probability of instances based on the intensity or the date of their or recent. In order to overcome the accessibility heuristic student should try to collect a variety of facts, take into consideration the statistical probability, and reevaluate their first impressions prior to reaching an.

The bias of anchoring is another cognitive bias that affects the way we make decisions. It is triggered when we are relying too much on the first data, which is often the initial thing we see to make subsequent judgements. In order to overcome this bias it is recommended that students practice suspending the initial judgements, collect the most relevant data feasible, and consider the various options available before making a decision upon a conclusion.

Additionally you can also identify the confirmation bias the availability heuristic as well as the anchoring bias, are only some of cognitive biases that affect our ability to critically think. It is crucial that students become conscious of their biases and to actively seek out ways to eliminate these. Through embracing a growth-oriented mindset by being open to different ideas, and continually challenging their assumptions they can improve their ability to think critically and create the conditions for the academic achievement they deserve.

The ability to overcome cognitive biases is a essential aspect to learning the art in critical thinking. Through recognizing and trying to overcome those biases, learners can increase their ability to be able to make informed choices, and analyze data objectively. By focusing on self-reflection and continuous practice learners can acquire the skills needed to be successful academically as well as beyond.

Developing Intellectual Humility

For academic excellence, developing the art of critical thinking is essential. The underlying principle of critical thinking is humbleness - the capacity to recognize the limits of our own understanding and to be open to other viewpoints. Intellectual humility isn't just essential to academic success as well as for professional and personal growth. In this chapter, we will discuss the importance of humility in intellectual life and will offer strategies for develop this quality.

Intellectual humility can be the solution to arrogance in the classroom, which could hinder progress in academics. Being humble in your thinking means accepting the fact that there's always more to be learned and that our individual beliefs and ideas cannot be trusted as absolute. The mindset of this type encourages curiosity learning, and real respect for different perspectives. Through recognizing the fact that knowledge changes constantly and that no one is able to answer all questions, students can establish a culture which promotes growth in their minds as well as collaboration.

To cultivate intellectual humility learners must develop curiosity. Instead of thinking they have all the information on a subject the students should tackle the subject with an open mind and the desire to continue learning. It's about actively searching for the latest information, participating in discussion with fellow students or professors, as well as embracing the discomfort of questioning one's beliefs.

An additional aspect that is essential to cultivating intelligence is to recognize and confronting one's own biases. There are many preconceived notions and biases which can impair our judgement and limit our ability to be able to think critically. In recognizing these biases, and actively pursuing different perspectives learners can increase their perspective on complex problems and build a more balanced and comprehensive method of problem solving.

Additionally, active listening and empathy could help to build the development of intellectual humility. When you are truly listening to people and trying to comprehend the perspectives of others, students are able to increase their understanding and gain an enlightened understanding of a range of topics. The empathetic way of thinking will not only improve the ability to think critically but encourages collaboration and effective communication.

Intellectual humility is a must to students who want to achieve academic success. Through acknowledging the limits of their own understanding and fostering curiosity, confronting prejudices, and using the art of active listening and empathy students will be able to unlock their potential as critically thinking individuals. A culture of humility and intellectual curiosity fosters a climate that encourages intellectual development, cooperation and respect for different viewpoints - essential elements for success in school as well as personal growth.

Embracing Curiosity

To achieve academic excellence, one aspect that is frequently overlooked curiosity.

Curiousness is the primary force of critical thinking, and it plays an important part in developing the abilities required for academic success. In this section we'll explore the significance of being curious and the ways it can improve the ability to think critically.

Curiosity refers to the desire to discover more, to inquire, and explore. It's the base of critical thinking because it encourages us to question our the assumptions of others, to analyze data, and take part in deep knowledge. Being curious as students will allow us to tackle the course by keeping an open mind and determined to explore new ideas and viewpoints.

One of the main positive effects of curiosity is the fact that it boosts the desire to learn. When we're enthusiastic about something is more inclined to put in the efforts and time into understanding the subject thoroughly. The desire to understand motivates us to seek out answers, do studies, and take part in the class discussion. Through embracing curiosity, you change the process of learning from an academic activity into an individual journey of discovering.

Engaging in curiosity can help us improve our critical thinking skills. In constant questioning and looking for solutions, we grow better at assessing facts, distinguishing between fact and opinion, as well as deciphering the logic of a fallacy. The pursuit of curiosity encourages people to think about our surroundings as well as to challenge the norm and develop your own perspectives.

Additionally, curiosity encourages creative thinking. If we tackle a challenge or a subject with an open-minded approach, you are more likely to come up with innovative ideas and solutions. Inquisitiveness stimulates our minds which allows people to think out of the boundaries and consider the possibilities of new ideas. Through embracing curiosity, we tap into the creative side of us and increase our capacity to face challenging academic issues.

To be willing to embrace curiosity, it's important to develop a habit that is open to learning throughout your life. That means being open fresh ideas, constantly looking for different perspectives and taking the initiative to question the assumptions we hold about ourselves. Also, it is important to be fascinated by learning and the process itself, asking us why we're doing it and how it relates to our own goals and the best way to apply the knowledge in real-world scenarios.

Being curious is vital to building critical thinking abilities and for achieving academic success. In fostering our natural need to discover and grow and discover, we increase our enthusiasm and improve our thinking capabilities, and unlock our creativity. Therefore, let curiosity serve as your guide towards academic top-quality. Be awed by it, cultivate it and let it guide the journey to lifelong studying.

Cultivating Open-Mindedness

In the current world of rapid change having a sharp mind is vital to the success of your academic career. The ability to think in a critical manner allows students to think critically, analyze data, analyze arguments and take informed choices. One of the key aspects in critical thinking usually gets overlooked is an open mind. It is the capacity to think about different viewpoints and new perspectives, and to challenge ones own assumptions. It's the most important factor in growing knowledge, fostering compassion, and encouraging the development of one's academic skills.

In order to foster an open mind to foster open-mindedness, students should first understand that it is important to embrace different perspectives. When they realize that their personal convictions and views are not true, they make the space to consider alternative viewpoints. This lets them approach conversations or debates in a manner that is characterized by curiosity, and respect, instead of defensiveness.

An effective method to increase an open mind is to expose students to diverse views and sources. Students must actively search for various perspectives when they read publications, articles as well as academic works from various disciplines and authors. Students should also participate in dialogue with peers as well as professors and specialists in different areas. In pursuing opposing perspectives, students will acquire a greater comprehension of the complex and improve their thinking abilities.

One of the most important aspects in developing curiosity is to challenge one's beliefs and prejudices. Students should be able to question their assumptions and think about different explanations. Self-reflection can help students recognize and eliminate cognitive biases that can hinder their ability to critically think. Through constantly reevaluating their assumptions, they can build an understanding that is more complex of difficult issues. They also become more open-minded.

In addition, encouraging open-mindedness involves taking the time to listen to people as well as considering their views. It is crucial to engage in discussions with respect and empathy and create a place in which everyone feels at ease expressing opinions. Engaging actively and listening in a thoughtful discussion students are able to broaden their perspective and gain new ideas.

Chapter 4: Effective Communication And Critical Thinking

Active Listening

To achieve academic success, a crucial ability that is often overlooked is listening actively. Students get bombarded by facts, either during lectures, in discussions or when we are reading our textbooks. But, simply hearing words spoken or reading the text on a paper is not enough. It is the act of taking the information effectively, that can greatly enhance our ability to critically think as well as overall academic performance.

The act of listening is more than simply being attentive to the spoken words. It involves being aware, processing mental details, and continuously trying for the meaning behind it. Through active listening to the message, we are able to gain valuable information, pinpoint key elements and connect them to other points which otherwise would be overlooked.

What can we do to develop a habit of listening? The first step is that it's important to get rid of distractions. Remove your mobile and close any unneeded tabs on your laptop You should also find a tranquil place where you can concentrate only on your task. Next, adopt a curious mindset. Engage in every conversation, lecture or book with an open mind to discovering things you have never heard of. It will allow you to remain engaged and search for knowledge.

An effective method of active listening is to make notes. Not only does this help you remember information, but also allows you to summarize, summarize and analyze critically the information you're hearing or writing. Make note-taking a system which is most effective for you such as notes, bullet points or a mix of both.

A key element of active listening is to ask questions. Do not be afraid to ask for clarification or go more deeply into a subject. It not only shows your interest but also improves the understanding of. When you ask questions, it is possible to will challenge the assumptions you have made, consider diverse perspectives and reveal undiscovered insights.

Active listening also extends beyond the schoolroom. Participate in discussions that are meaningful among your professors, peers as well as your mentors. Make sure you are active in your listening while working on studies or group projects. When you are actively listening to a variety of views and opinions and perspectives, you will be able to broaden your understanding of yourself and build the ability to think more broadly critically thought.

It is essential to have active listening capability to be successful in school. When we eliminate distracting factors, adopting a more curious attitude, taking notes and asking questions and engaging in meaningful discussion to become proficient and effective learners. The act of listening improves the ability to think critically as well as helps us remember knowledge, and enhances the overall performance of our academics. Let us try to improve our listening skills and learn the art in critical thinking.

Constructive Questioning

Subchapter: Constructive Questioning

To achieve success in school, mastering the ability to think critically is essential. Critical thinking enables students to examine information, assess arguments, and come to sensible choices. The most fundamental element to be considered in critical thinking constructive questions. This chapter explores the importance of constructive questions and the ways it could improve students' ability to think critically.

Questioning with constructive intent involves asking well-thought out and intelligent questions that stimulate more understanding and reflection. It forces students to rethink their the assumptions they have made, to evaluate evidence and consider different viewpoints. Through engaging in constructive discussion it allows students to broaden their horizons of thinking and gain an understanding that is more complex of the subject.

One of the main advantages of asking questions constructively is that it can foster curiosity and interest. Students who are actively asking questions about what they're studying will be more likely to show an interest that is genuine in their subject. Through asking questions continuously and seeking out answers they become actively involved in their education and acquire a passion to learn.

The practice of constructive questioning plays an important role in the development of the ability to think critically. Students who ask questions are they're asked to consider the material they are presented with. They discover the gaps in their knowledge as well as evaluate the veracity of the sources and think about other perspectives. Through this process, students to develop into more critical and thinkers who are able to make informed decisions.

Furthermore, honest questions are essential to effective solution-finding. Through asking thoughtful questions students can help reduce complex issues into smaller pieces, which will allow an organized approach to solving problems. Students are able to identify their basic assumptions, analyze the reliability of data, and think about alternative solutions. It is this ability to critically consider and to ask the right questions can be extremely useful for academic and practical scenario.

To cultivate constructive questioning skills, students can employ various strategies. This could include engaging in discussion with their classmates and seeking clarification whenever it is unclear, challenging the beliefs and assumptions they have about themselves as well as engaging in their own studies to examine different points of view.

The ability to ask questions constructively is an important component to mastering critical thinking in order to be successful academically. In encouraging students to consider their concerns and ask questions to their questions, it increases their interest as well as develops the ability to think critically and encourages problem-solving. Students who engage in constructive questions are active learners who are competent in analyzing information as well as evaluating arguments and taking sound choices. When they integrate constructive questioning in their educational journeys students will be able to unlock their potential to the fullest and attain the success they desire in their academic pursuits.

Presenting Arguments Persuasively

For the academic world Critical thinking abilities play crucial roles in shaping the ability to think critically as well as evaluate and articulate arguments effectively. In order to achieve excellence as a student must master the art of presenting arguments which draws attention, captivates viewers, and finally persuades them to accept your position. This chapter aims at providing readers with the required equipment and methods to be able to master the art of convincing argumentation.

In the beginning, it is vital to build an underlying foundation to the arguments you make. It involves doing extensive research, gathering pertinent data, and critically reviewing diverse perspectives on the issue that you are tackling. When you do this you'll be able to bolster your arguments and anticipate any counter arguments, strengthening your overall argument.

When you've collected your facts, it's crucial to structure your arguments in a rational and logical manner. Introduce your argument with a concise that gives background and establishes the scene to present your arguments. Make use of this chance to capture your audience's attention. Clearly present your argument and define the key aspects you'll address.

Additionally, to communicate your argument persuasively It is essential to draw the attention of the emotions and beliefs of the viewers. Through the use of powerful stories, appropriate scenarios, and relatable narratives to create an emotional connection with your audience and make your argument more relevant and convincing. Furthermore, using rhetorical tools like similes, metaphors, and powerful language could help create an appealing picture to people who read your content and increase your persuasiveness that your claims make.

Additionally, confronting arguments that are counterproductive and effectively refuting them is an essential aspect of convincing arguments. Recognizing the opposing views shows the integrity of your thinking and strengthens your argument. In a respectful manner, you can debunk arguments using solid evidence and logic demonstrate your ability to be a critical thinker and build credibility among your readers.

A persuasive argument needs a solid and confident presentation. Learn to improve your presentation skills keep eye contact and employ proper body language to connect with your viewers. Make sure you are aware of your voice and ensure that it is professional and respectful throughout the entire.

Effectively presenting arguments is an essential skill to students who want to achieve academic success. Conducting thorough study, structuring your arguments in a rational manner and appealing to the emotions of your audience as well as tackling counter arguments, and being confident in your presentation and confidence, you will master the art of convincing argumentation. Keep in mind that being able to make arguments convincingly persuasive does not just improve your performance in school but gives you a lifetime ability to use it in a myriad of professional and personal scenarios.

Engaging in Collaborative DiscussionsCollaborative discussions play a crucial role in the development of critical thinking skills for academic success. Students often encounter ourselves engaged in group projects or participating in discussions with our classmates as well as participating in studies groups. The collaborative tasks provide valuable opportunities to develop the capacity to think critically and aid in the overall development of our academics.

One of the major advantages of having conversations with others is exposure to different perspectives and thoughts. In working with other people are exposed to different views as well as experiences and information that expand our knowledge of the subject. When we are actively listening to colleagues and examining their viewpoints and perspectives, we are able to critically think and analyze various perspectives prior to forming our own thoughts.

In addition, collaboration discussions promote active participation as well as effective communications skills. Through these discussions allow us to articulate your thoughts in a concise and clear manner and back up our ideas by proving them, and respectably contest the ideas of others. These interactions not only help us improve the ability to think critically, as well as prepares us for our future professional and academic tasks where effective communication is crucial.

Engaging in discussion with others encourages collaboration and teamwork. When we are in a group you learn how to collaborate, share jobs, and draw on the strengths of each other. Participating actively in these discussions, we increase the capacity to work effectively and solve issues collectively and reach the same targets. These abilities are extremely sought-after in educational settings and will prove invaluable when we enter our professional careers.

In order to make the most of collaboration, it's important to conduct the discussions with a wide-ranging mind and willingness to gain knowledge from other people. Be attentive to the opinions of your colleagues and ask questions with a thoughtful approach and give constructive comments. Take care to be respectful and understanding of the views of others regardless of whether they are different from the ones you hold. The goal isn't to win the argument, but rather to participate in meaningful discussions of ideas, which encourages the development of critical thinking and academic excellence.

Involving in group discussions is a crucial element in mastering critical thinking to achieve academic success. Participating actively in discussions with peers students gain different perspectives, improve their communication abilities, and build effective teamwork skills. Engaging in collaboration will add to the overall development of our academics and put us on a way to be successful in our academics and in the future.

Writing Clearly and Coherently

In today's frantic academic environment it is essential to be able to write effectively and in a coherent manner is essential to achieving your goals. If you're writing an essay, research paper or an easy class project the writing abilities you have are crucial to the effective communication of your ideas and achieving the marks you want. The chapter will focus on how important it is to write in a clear and concise manner, with tips and tricks that will help you improve this crucial skill.

In the first place, clarity and coherence in writing are vital to communicate effectively. When you express your ideas in a clear and concise manner, readers will quickly comprehend and follow your thought process. This is crucial in academic writing. Your classmates and your professors depend on your writing to be able to grasp and understand the arguments you make. When you write clearly, you prove your knowledge of your subject and increase your standing as a thoughtful thinker.

For clarity when writing To write with clarity, you must plan your ideas logically. The first step is to outline your principal thoughts and citing evidence prior to beginning the writing procedure. This can help ensure that your structure is clear and make sure that every paragraph adds to the overall flow of your essay. In addition, you can use the words and phrases that transition that help readers navigate your arguments in a fluid manner.

A further important aspect of writing with clarity is to use simple and clear the language. Do not use jargons or confusing sentences that can make your readers confused. Try to focus on simplicity and clarity, by using phrases that clearly convey your intention. Keep in mind that writing clearly doesn't mean reducing the ideas you have in mind;

it's that you present them in a way which is easy to comprehend by your readers.

Additionally the editing and proofreading process is a crucial step to achieving consistency and clarity in your writing. Make sure to check and revise your piece for punctuation, grammar as well as spelling mistakes. Also, look for logic errors and make sure your argument flows smoothly between paragraphs and the following. Examining feedback from other students or using writing centers could be a great source of information on those areas that require attention.

The ability to communicate clearly and effectively is essential to academic achievement. If you organize your thoughts in logical ways by using clear and concise terminology, and thoroughly checking your work for errors will enhance the ability of communicating effectively and prove your ability to master the process of critical thinking. Be aware that clear writing is not just beneficial to your academic accomplishments, but it also provides the basis for efficient communication across a range of situations, both personal and professional. Make sure you invest the your time and energy into mastering this art and benefit during your college experience and beyond.

Chapter 5: Applying Critical Thinking In Different Academic Disciplines

Critical Thinking in Science and Mathematics

Math and Science are two areas that need the foundational knowledge of critical thinking to ensure academic performance. While studying these subjects there is no need to merely memorize facts or formulas. Instead, students should engage in a process of critically thinking to understand and use the ideas. In this subchapter we'll explore the significance of critical thinking in mathematics and science and offer strategies for enhancing the skills of these students.

Science requires critical thinking. It is the process of analyzing, questioning, as well as evaluating evidence. It's about being open and skeptical, posing probing questions and obtaining arguments to prove or debunk assertions. In the field of science, critical thinking aids students to develop theories, develop experiments and analyze information. They can establish connections between various concepts and theories, and to recognize patterns and patterns. Without the ability to think critically the students might struggle to comprehend the basic concepts and might not be able to use their knowledge efficiently.

Critical maths thinking requires more than understanding formulas and solving equations. Students must consider their thinking logically, think abstractly and look at issues from many perspectives. Thinking critically about mathematics helps students to identify patterns, understand relationships and draw connections between various math notions. They can analyze their issues, develop strategies and use the right techniques to solve problems. Without the ability to think critically learners may be unable to tackle complex challenges and could rely in memorization based on the rote, which leads to poor understanding and lack of retention.

To build critical thinking abilities in mathematics and science, students may employ a variety of methods. An effective method is to pose questions. Students should be encouraged to ask questions about the reasons and what, as well as to ask for clarification and challenge beliefs. The students should be taught how to critically analyze data examine its credibility, and take a look at multiple viewpoints. Students should be encouraged to consider their ideas and come up with alternatives to solve problems. Engaging in debates, discussions or group projects will also help develop abilities to think critically as it encourages students to look at various perspectives and to argue for themselves.

Teachers can also offer real-world applications and examples of mathematical and scientific ideas to illustrate the importance and significance of thinking critically. Inviting students to tackle unsolved problems, and to engage with hands-on activities can improve their critical thinking abilities. Teachers must give constructive feedback and assist students as they reflect about their thinking processes as well as ways to solve problems.

Skills for critical thinking are crucial to academic success in math and science. Inspiring students to ask questions how they analyze, think about, and assess knowledge will not only enhance their knowledge, but also help students to use their knowledge efficiently. In fostering the ability to think critically learners will be stronger problem solvers, enduring learners and discerning consumers of information on these topics.

Critical Thinking in Humanities and Social Sciences

In the current world of rapid change Critical thinking is an essential aspect of academic achievement. It is no more crucial than in the areas of the humanities and social sciences where analysis of critical nature and evaluation are crucial aspects of academic work. This chapter focuses on the role of critical thinking in these areas by exploring ways it can help you learn more as well as contribute to the overall development of your academic career.

The social and humanities cover diverse subjects, such as the fields of sociology, literature, history as well as psychology and the study of politics, to name a few. Although each field has distinct methods and approaches but they are united by the requirement to think critically. Through the process of critical thinking, you will be competent to tackle complex problems and texts with an empathetic eyes, allowing you to discern significance, assess arguments and make well-considered decisions.

One of the fundamental elements of critical thinking within the sciences of humanities and social is the capacity to analyse and understand texts. It doesn't matter if it's an historical document or literary masterpiece or a sociological analysis the ability of critical thinking enables one to go beyond the superficial and discover the deeper implications and meanings. When you examine the intentions of the author as well as their biases and larger historical and cultural background, you will be able to develop an understanding that is more complex of the issue.

Additionally, critical thinking within these areas involves the weighing of evidence and arguments. When you study social and humanities are likely to encounter numerous views and theories. Critical thinking lets you evaluate the credibility of these theories, analyzing the data presented, and then identifying the logic flaws and prejudices. Through this it is possible to build an informed and well-rounded view which allows you to be able to participate in meaningful debates in the academic field.

Additionally, critical thinking within social and human sciences encourages an interdisciplinarity method of thinking. The fields are often interconnected with each other, and through the use of the skills of critical thinking will allow you to make connections among different disciplines, as well as integrate multiple viewpoints. This type of thinking stimulates imagination and creativity, which allows the development of new ideas and aid in the development of knowledge in these fields.

To develop the ability to think critically within the humanities and social sciences, it's vital to actively engage with the content. It is about challenging the assumptions of others, seeking out alternative perspectives and engaging in deep analysis. Furthermore, acquiring effective communicating skills, both writing as well as oral, is essential in order to express your ideas and participate an engaging academic discussion.

The end result is that learning to think critically in the social and human sciences is not just a way to increase your academic performance, but will also provide you with the necessary skills to ensure your continued career advancement. If you can become a critically-minded person and a critical thinker, you'll be able to deal with the complexity of the world, analyze the information you receive critically and make a contribution to the world by contributing in a thoughtful and informed approach.

Critical Thinking in Business and Economics

In the current competitive environment the ability to think critically is crucial to success in academics especially in the areas of economics and business. Ability to analyse as well as evaluate and interpret data critically is essential for students who wish to be successful in these fields. This chapter aims at providing students with a thorough knowledge that critical thinking skills can be utilized effectively in the fields of business as well as economics.

One of the primary elements that is critical in the fields of business as well as economics is to take informed decisions that are based on thorough analysis. When it comes to these areas, the decisions usually involve complex information that have financial implications and possible risks. Through developing their thinking abilities learners can determine the accuracy and validity of information, recognize weaknesses, and assess the possible outcomes from different plans of decision making. It allows them to take well-considered, informed decision-making, which is crucial for economic and business environment.

Additionally the critical thinking process in the fields of economics and business requires applying logical thinking in problem-solving. The students must understand the root cause of challenges, consider a variety of solutions, and then evaluate their strengths and limitations. Through critical thinking, they are able to develop creative and efficient solutions for real-world business or economic issues.

Additionally, the ability to think critically can be crucial in understanding and comprehending economic concepts, theories and ideas. In the fields of economics and business students often have to evaluate and analyze the economic theory and its practical effects. Utilizing their critical thinking skills students are able to evaluate the legitimacy and validity of the theory, recognize flaws in the argument and evaluate critically the proofs that back them.

Critical thinking, in the field of economics and business involves communication skills efficiently. The students must communicate their ideas, provide the evidence they need to prove their points and participate in productive discussions. Critical thinking allows students to communicate their thoughts effectively, convincingly and in a structured manner improving their capability to be successful academically.

Critical thinking is a crucial capability for students who are pursuing academic success in the areas of economics and business. When they develop the ability to think critically learners can make educated decisions, tackle complex problems learn about economic concepts, and effectively communicate. Learning to think critically in the fields of economics and business can not only improve academic performance, but also equip students to succeed in their career paths.

Critical Thinking in Arts and Literature

For those studying in the field of academia Critical thinking abilities are crucial to success across all fields of study. From science to humanities, the ability analyze critically enables students to think critically as well as evaluate arguments and formulate well-thought-out views. But when you're talking about literature and the arts Critical thinking acquires an important role.

Literature and the arts provide a vast array of concepts perspective, feelings, and emotions to students. If it's analysing a novel and decoding a symbolism painting, or decoding an instrument Critical thinking is essential to comprehending and appreciating these artistic art forms.

One of the fundamental features of critical thinking within the fields of literature and art is the ability to dig past the surface. This involves going beyond the initial impressions, and examining the meanings underneath. In the case of you read a book Critical thinkers look at the writer's usage of language themes, plots, and character advancement to obtain greater understanding of the novel.

Furthermore, critical analysis in literature and arts is closely tied to the interpretation and analysis. Students are encouraged to consider the motives behind characters, study the context of culture and history of a work as well as discern the writer's intention behind the piece. Through this kind of study, they develop the ability to construct well-founded arguments as well as defend their opinions.

Additionally, critical thinking in literature and arts fosters imagination and imagination. The students are challenged to look outside of the box and challenge the norms of traditional thought and consider alternative viewpoints. Through critical analysis of the work of other artists, they can discover their own creative voice and participate in an ongoing discussion in the art world.

To improve the critical thinking skills in literature and arts students are able to engage with a range of different exercises. This could include taking part in discussion groups, visiting shows of art or creating analytical essays. Also, exploring various genres and media can help broaden an comprehension and appreciation for a variety of art forms.

Skills in critical thinking are essential to academic success in every discipline, and the literature and the arts are not an one-offs. When they develop the ability of their brains to think critically learners can discover the depths hidden in artistic works, analyze their meaning with some nuance, and participate in the current debate across these disciplines.

Take advantage of the strength of critical thinking within the realms of literature and art Let your creativity fly.

Critical Thinking in Health Sciences

:

The health science field has many complex issues and constantly evolving technological advancements. In order to navigate the ever-changing landscape with ease, students studying the field of health sciences should acquire strong critical thinking skills. In this chapter we'll look at the role of critical thinking in the health sciences and ways that it could aid your academic progress. If you master critical thinking and analyzing information, you'll be able to analyse information, make well-informed decisions and be able to contribute effectively in the area.

Why Critical Thinking Matters in Health Sciences:

Critical thinking is at the heart of sound decision-making within medical sciences. It requires examining data without bias, challenging assumptions as well as drawing logical connections. In this area where lives are in the balance and the accuracy of diagnosis is crucial the ability to think critically is crucial. Through acquiring these abilities will make you an expert healthcare professional who is adept at tackling difficult medical issues and providing the best treatment to patients.

Developing Critical Thinking Skills:

For you to be successful in the sciences of health, you need to develop your thinking skills. This means establishing specific habits and devising methods that improve the analytical skills of your students. A good example is exploring different viewpoints. When you consider different viewpoints and perspectives, you will be able to develop an understanding of health issues and come up with creative strategies. Also, focusing on reflection and self-awareness allows you to discover and eliminate any preconceived beliefs or prejudices that could hinder the process of critical thinking.

Applying Critical Thinking in Health Sciences:

Critical thinking doesn't just apply to class discussions or assignments It extends to real-world health care environments. Students need to actively search for occasions to use your thinking abilities. Take part in case studies, take part in debates, and participate in group discussions. This will enhance the ability of you to evaluate the complexities of medical issues, consider data, and make educated decision-making.

Chapter 6: Strategies For Problem-Solving And Decision Making

Defining the Problem

When we attempt to learn the technique of critical thinking, it is vital to begin with understanding the importance of defining the issue. The chapter will explore all elements of problem definition, and its importance in academic achievement.

Students frequently face difficult problems that demand thinking skills and analytical abilities. Before we can tackle any issue it is essential to first comprehend and clearly define the problem. This first step establishes the stage for analytical thinking, and makes sure that all efforts focussed and focused.

The definition of the problem requires us to identify the main issue or concern in question. This requires breaking complicated problems down into manageable pieces that allow us to analyse and comprehend the issues more efficiently. When we define the issue it is possible to narrow the focus of our analysis and not waste the time and effort on unnecessary factors.

A common error students commit is believing that the issue is obvious or settling for a simplistic description without further investigation. But, critical thinking requires an in-depth understanding and analysis of the issue's origins and the scope. Through asking questions and obtaining more information, we are able to find hidden layers of complexity and get an understanding of the problem from a greater perspective.

In addition, the process of defining the problem is a matter of considering various perspectives and theories. It forces people to consider the issue from a different perspective and test our beliefs as well as biases. Through engaging in diverse viewpoints We increase our capacity to look at problems from various perspectives. This leads to better-rounded and more intelligent strategies.

For a clear definition of a problem it is possible to employ various strategies like the mind map, brainstorming or even conducting a studies. These tools allow us to gather details, examine different dimensions and uncover any root concerns that were ignored in the beginning. With these tools will ensure that the problem is defined in a thorough manner and precise.

In the end, understanding how to define a problem is vital to the success of your academic career. If we can master this ability, we will be able to take on academic challenges with a clear and focused approach and ensure that we address the correct problem and come up with solidly-thought out strategies. Furthermore, this ability goes beyond academics to prepare us for the difficulties we might face both in our professional and personal life.

Determining the root of the issue is the most important first step to learning the art in critical thinking. When we are able to pinpoint the primary problem, examining multiple angles using effective methods that allow us to navigate difficult problems with ease and attain the academic excellence we desire. Therefore, let's go into this adventure of thinking critically, equipped with the capability to identify issues and unleash our potential.

Analyzing Different Perspectives

In the current complex and connected world, the ability to think critically and analyze multiple perspectives is an essential skill to ensure the academic achievement. In our studies, we frequently encounter a myriad of ideas, theories and theories in our studies which is why being able analyze them critically is crucial to develop a broad comprehension of any subject. This chapter will discuss how important it is to analyze various perspectives, and offer practical ways to improve the ability to think critically.

One of the most important reason to consider various perspectives is to stay away from getting caught in the trap of narrow-mindedness. If we just consider one view or rely on one source of knowledge, we are missing the vastness and depth of the subject of discussion. If we actively seek out various perspectives we are able to gain a thorough understanding of the issue that is at hand. This is not just a sign of an interest in the subject but also permits participants to participate in a more thoughtful debate and discussions.

Additionally, considering different perspectives helps us develop into more conscious thinkers. This encourages us to ask questions, think critically, question beliefs, and consider the facts that support different arguments. When we are exposed to a variety of perspectives it improves our capacity to make independent and informed decisions. This is not just important in the academic setting but is also useful in our work as well as personal daily lives.

For a successful analysis of different perspectives in a meaningful manner, we must be able to approach this process by keeping an open mind. It is essential to put aside our preconceptions and openly listen to different views, even when they do not align with our views. Engaging in a respectful conversation with those who are of diverse opinions may expand our perspectives and allow us to develop an understanding that is more complex of the issue.

Furthermore, it is crucial to examine the authenticity and veracity of the various viewpoints. All sources of information are made equal. Students need to assess the validity of the data as well as the experience of the writer or speaker and the potential for conflict of interest or biases. The process of evaluating will allow students to differentiate between well-backed arguments and those that are not supported by sufficient evidence.Analyzing various views is essential to be successful in academics. When we are actively seeking out different views, examining assumptions and critically reviewing evidence, you can develop your ability to think critically. This ability will not only increase our performance in school but will also help us traverse the maze of our world and make well-informed choices. Therefore, let's take up the challenge of considering various perspectives, and begin a an adventure to become intelligent, well-rounded individuals.

Generating Possible Solutions

For academic success, critical-thinking is a crucial aspect. The most important component to be considered in critical thinking is its ability to come up with solutions for the challenges and problems faced by students during their educational journey. This chapter aims at providing students with the most effective methods to improve their problem solving skills and come up with creative strategies.

When confronted with a dilemma It is crucial to approach the issue with an open-minded and creative approach. If you are able to think outside the norm, students are able to think of a range of possible solutions that aren't immediately evident. The chapter will lead students in a sequential process to let their imaginations run wild and develop new concepts.

The first step towards generating potential solutions is to fully comprehend the issue. Students must look at the issue from multiple perspectives, focusing on its root reasons and possible implications. The knowledge gained will serve as an excellent foundation to create practical solutions.

When students are able to get a good understanding of the issue, they are able to use brainstorming methods to come up with a variety of ideas. Brainstorming is a way to encourage free-flowing, non-judgmental thinking. It allows students to consider a broad variety of possibilities without limiting. In this chapter, students will learn about various methods of brainstorming, such as mind mapping, listing and group brainstorming. It will allow students to use their imagination and come up with a variety of strategies.

Once they've compiled a list with possibilities, students have be able to assess and rank these. It is important to consider the viability of each solution, its practicality, as well as the potential consequences of each option. When they critically evaluate the benefits and drawbacks of each solution the students will be able to narrow their options, and pick those that are most feasible.

Additionally, this chapter will highlight that collaboration plays a crucial role as well as looking for perspectives from different angles. Students will be taught the importance to engage with colleagues or professors as well as experts in order to get valuable insight and develop their ideas. Through actively soliciting feedback and suggestions from other students Students can improve their concepts and increase their ability to solve problems.

Ability to think of potential solutions is an essential element of the critical thinking abilities in order to be successful academically. The subchapter provides students with the required methods and tools to tackle issues with a fresh perspective, think out of the box and come up with creative solutions. Through mastering the art of coming up with feasible solutions, students will increase their ability to solve problems as well as increase their creativity and then succeed in their academic pursuits.

Evaluating and Selecting the Best Solution

For academic excellence the ability to think critically plays an important role. As students, we're continually confronted by challenges and challenges that demand the ability to think through and come up with the best solution. This chapter guides readers through looking over and deciding on the most effective solution. It will also equip students with the tools needed for success in academic pursuits.

In the event of a situation When faced with a problem, the first thing to do is to look at the issue and determine the best solution. This will require a deep knowledge of the issue in hand as well as the capacity to think imaginatively. When you consider multiple viewpoints as well as brainstorming your ideas it is possible to broaden possibilities and improve chances of finding the most efficient solution.

When you've created the list of alternatives Next stage is to assess every one of them using the guidelines. Examine the practicality, feasibility as well as potential benefits for each option. Consider questions like What is the likelihood of success for this approach? Does it tackle the root of the issue? What are the advantages and risks? If you take a critical look at each choice and narrowing the options available and concentrate on the ones that have the best chance to be successful.

While evaluating options, you need to think about the ethical consequences that your decisions have. As students, we are held to an obligation to make moral choices that are in line with our beliefs and ethics of academic ethics. Consider the consequences of every solution for your own, other people, and your community as a whole. So, you can be sure that the choice of solution doesn't just address the issue, but also adheres to the ethical code of conduct.

After careful analysis It is now the right time to pick the ideal option. It requires trust in your judgment-making skills and the courage to risk your life. Rely on your skills of critical thinking and accept the possibility of failing since it's through mistakes which we can learn and improve. Be aware that choosing the right option may not bring immediate results however it can put your on the road to constant improvement and excellence in your academics.

If you can master the art of looking at and choosing the right solution, you'll acquire analytical skills which are crucial to your learning success. The skills you acquire extend beyond the school, and allow individuals to tackle problems with confidence and discover creative solutions to all areas of your lives. Be open to this process, trust your intuition, and unleash your potential as an intelligent thinking person.

Implementing and Assessing the Chosen Solution

When you've critically assessed the issue and come up with the solution you want to pursue The next process is to implement and evaluate the solution you have chosen. The chapter will lead through this procedure by equipping you with required skills needed to make sure that your selected solution is successfully executed and then evaluated on its performance.

Implementing a solution demands meticulous planning and implementation. Begin by breaking your solution into small achievable tasks. Make a schedule and establish reasonable goals for tracking the progress you make. Ask for help from sources, like instructors, experts or your classmates. They can offer valuable advice and assistance throughout the process of implementation.

Communication is essential for successful execution. It is essential to clearly communicate the idea as well as the intended results to every stakeholder involved. This can help get their cooperation and support and increase the likelihood of an efficient execution. Inform stakeholders regularly about how things are progressing and resolve any issues or concerns that might arise on the process.

After the solution is put into place, it's crucial to determine its efficiency. It will give valuable information on whether or not it has actually solved the issue that is being addressed. Comprehensive evaluations include analyzing both the unintended and intended effects that the proposed solution has.

To evaluate the proposed solution take into consideration collecting data using diverse methods, such as surveys, interviews or even direct observation. These techniques will enable you to evaluate the effect of the solution, and also find areas of improvement. Use your the ability to think examine the data you've obtained and create meaningful sketches.

Be aware that the evaluation of your chosen option is a continuous process. Always monitor the effectiveness of your solution and then make any necessary adjustments. The ability to think critically plays a vital roles during the evaluation process and will allow you to spot weaknesses or flaws and suggest alternative options in the event of a need.

When you implement and evaluate the solution you choose by implementing and evaluating the solution, you're actively participating in the academic process accomplishment through an ability to think critically. These abilities not only allow you to resolve problems with ease but they also help you build a an excellent foundation to build upon for your future activities. Take advantage of the chance to develop and develop your skills of critical thinking that will help you succeed in your studies.

Implementation and evaluation of your chosen method is a crucial step to develop critical thinking to achieve academic success. When you carefully plan, effectively communicating, and continually assessing to increase the chance of to solve the issue. Accept the challenges associated when implementing solutions and reviewing them to become the master of critical thinking and pave the way to success in academics and even greater success.

Chapter 7: Overcoming Challenges In Critical Thinking

Becoming aware of and dealing with cognitive Biases

In the current world of rapid change in which information is easily available to all of us It is essential that students develop abilities to use critical thinking in order to get across the ocean of information. A key aspect of critical thinking is to be aware of and dealing cognitive biases.

Cognitive biases can be a result of flaws within our thought processes which could lead to mistakes in judgement and decision-making. They are usually due to our brains having shortcuts in order to make decisions quickly but they could limit our ability to think objectively and critically. Students who are striving to achieve academic success, it's important to recognize the biases that can be a problem and to learn to minimize their effect.

The most common cognitive bias we face is the confirmation bias. It tends to look to find, analyze, favour or recall data that supports our assumptions or theories. The bias may prevent us from looking at alternative perspectives and hinder our ability to consider the world in a critical manner. To combat confirmation bias students need to actively look for various sources of information. They should test their beliefs, and open themselves to other views.

A different common mistake is the availability heuristic in which we are reliant on the quick examples that spring to minds when making decisions or making decisions. This can cause us to underestimate the probability of occurrences or circumstances which are easy to recall as well as underestimating situations that don't stick in our minds. In order to counteract the heuristic of availability learners should aim to collect comprehensive and trustworthy facts prior to drawing or taking choices.

Anchoring bias is another cognitive bias that influences our thought processes. It is a result of relying too much on the initial element of data we are presented with in making judgements or estimations. The bias may limit the ability of us to think about the other information that is relevant and could result in inaccurate conclusions. The students should be cognizant of the bias in anchoring and search for more information prior to choosing a specific view or method of solving a problem.

Being aware of and managing cognitive biases is a crucial capability for success in academics. Through gaining self-awareness and confronting our own biases and biases, we will be able to increase our ability to think critically and make better informed choices. It is essential to look at data objectively, consider various perspectives, and open to rethinking the assumptions we make about ourselves. When we do this we will improve our learning as well as problem solvers within the world of academia as well as beyond.

Managing Time and Prioritizing Tasks

Today's hectic world the ability to manage time and tasks prioritizing are crucial abilities for those who want to achieve academic performance. Being able to manage time and prioritize work isn't just essential for finishing assignments in a timely manner however, it can also improve the ability to think critically, increases self-control, and decreases the stress level. This chapter aims at providing students with strategies that are practical and methods to improve these competencies and be successful at their academic goals.

One of the most important aspects of managing time is to understand the importance of time. The time we have is limited which means that once gone, it is not able to be recovered. When they realize the value of their time, they can establish a sense that they are in a hurry and prioritize their work according to. In order to achieve this you must prepare a calendar or a task checklist that lists all projects and tasks with precise dates. When they visualize these assignments they can plan their time in a way that ensures that there are no crucial tasks forgotten.

A different method of controlling time is to use the idea to "chunking." This is the process of breaking down larger projects into smaller, manageable chunks. If you divide a complicated project into smaller chunks it allows students to work on them in a single step which reduces the feelings of overwhelming and increasing their efficiency. It is also essential to pinpoint the times that require maximum concentration and focus, and then assign those periods to harder work. This will not only increase efficiency but also helps with more efficient retention and absorption of knowledge.

In order to effectively prioritize work Students must be able to distinguish the important from urgent assignments. Important tasks require urgent attention. However, critical tasks can contribute to longer-term targets and a successful. When they understand the distinction and the importance of each task, students are able to prioritize them according to their importance and timeframes. Furthermore, it's important to be able to be able to say "no" to non-essential tasks or other activities that can slow progress toward the academic objectives. Set boundaries and avoiding distractions are vital to successful time control.

Furthermore, it's important to keep in mind that managing time does not just concern productivity and taking care of yourself. Students must make some time to relaxation, rest as well as recreation in order to keep the balance of work and personal life. Breaks and things that help to refresh the mind could actually increase efficiency and enhance the ability to think critically.

Through mastering how to manage their time and prioritizing their tasks Students can improve their academic results, decrease the stress level, and also develop crucial critical thinking abilities. Implementing the techniques outlined in this chapter will allow students to get the most out of their time, meet their academic objectives and open the door towards a prosperous future.

Overcoming Procrastination

Procrastination is an issue which many students have to face during their educational journey. It's the practice of putting off or putting off activities, resulting in tension, poor timing management and subpar academic results. But, with the proper techniques and mental attitude students can break this habit and learn the technique of critical thinking to ensure academic success.

1. Find the root cause the first step to getting rid of procrastination is identifying the root causes. This could include the fear of failing or lack of motivation or being overwhelmed by the job to be completed. When they recognize these issues the students are able to address them successfully and formulate a plan to conquer the challenges.

2. Establish clear goals: Having specific, achievable goals is crucial to end the habit of procrastination. Reduce larger tasks into manageable, smaller sections, and then set dates for each step. This strategy does not just make the task less overwhelming, but also offers satisfaction with every step completed.

3. Plan and prioritize: Effective time management is essential to achievement in school. Sort tasks according to their priority and urgency. Then, develop a calendar or a task list. It helps your students remain well-organized, focused and keeps work from getting piled up.

4. Remove Distractions: Find and remove distractions that can interfere with productivity. Remove notifications from your smartphone, locate an area to study in peace avoid the urge to use social media for entertainment or take part in activities that are not academic while studying.

5. Break tasks down into smaller chunks The task of completing a large amount can become too overwhelming and cause delay. Make them break down into smaller, easier to manage chunks. This makes work seem easier but also helps you achieve better concentration and better work.

6. Resolving to put off work demands self-discipline, determination and discipline. Learn to control your mind and avoid the temptation to put off tasks through self-control exercises and establishing your own routine. Start small then gradually increase your capacity to remain in a state of concentration for long durations.

7. Find Support: It could help to ask for help from your family, friends or mentors that can be accountable to you and offer support. Participating in study groups or locating your study partner can aid in staying focused and stay on the right course.

Through these techniques by implementing these strategies, students will be able to overcome their procrastination, and realize their full potential for critical thinking to achieve academic achievement. Keep in mind that getting rid of procrastination always a process that takes perseverance and determination. Through practice, time and a positive outlook learners can improve their methods of managing their time, increase their ability to think critically and attain high academic standards.

Handling the the influx of information

In the current fast-paced world of digital technology the students are continuously confronted with an overwhelming amount of data. From research and academic reports to news articles and social media feeds as well as emails, it can be difficult to understand and understand everything. This chapter is designed to provide students with strategies that are effective to manage the overload of information and to develop critical thinking abilities to be successful in their academic pursuits.

1. Sort and filter out information One of the most important steps to reduce the burden of information is to determine what information is important to your academic objectives. Remove irrelevant or less important details, like Facebook notifications and focus on items specifically related to your study. This helps reduce the feeling of being bombarded with data.

2. Learn effective strategies for reading Learn effective reading strategies: Reading is an essential knowledge for children, but it's also time-consuming. In order to deal with the overwhelming amount of information master the ability to skim look through texts quickly to identify crucial points, major arguments and proof. Also, you can practice active reading with the help of annotating, summarizing and asking questions that will help you be able to effectively engage with the text.

3. Find reliable sources: Given the wealth of information available online, it's vital to

discern between trusted and untrustworthy sources. Utilize the academic databases, scholarly journals as well as reputable sites to find well-studied and peer-reviewed content. With reliable sources, students can be sure of that they are getting the correct and reliable information. their information.

4. Organise and control data: Use efficient note-taking techniques to manage and keep track of important information. It doesn't matter if you're using bullet points or mind maps, or even digital apps like Evernote Find a strategy which is most suitable for your needs. The ability to break down complicated details into manageable pieces will assist you in processing and storing crucial points.

5. Develop critical thinking skills: Learning critical thinking abilities is necessary in order to make sense of the information overload. Examine and analyze the data that you encounter by examining the sources of information, its validity and assumptions. Examine different viewpoints and consider

evidence that can help form informed opinions. The ability to think critically helps students be able to make informed decisions and make decisions from a thorough knowledge of the subject.

6. Make breaks, and do self-care. The overload of information can drain your mind. It is essential to take periodic breaks, participate with physical exercise, as well as practice self-care methods like mindfulness or exercise for relaxation. Maintaining your health can improve your concentration and ability to effectively process information.

With these techniques using these methods, students are able to traverse the sea of data and acquire the skills of critical thinking essential for success in school. Keep in mind that the process of critical thinking doesn't solely about the consumption of information. It is additionally, it involves evaluating, synthesizing the information and utilizing it to a practical way. Begin to incorporate these strategies in your studies and you will see your ability to deal with information overload increase.

Developing Resilience in the Face of Failure

It is inevitable to fail in the course of our lives, particularly with regard to studies. It's not our failures which define our character, but how we deal with these failures. To achieve academic success, cultivating resilience is an essential skill that will help us to overcome obstacles, make amends from mistakes and eventually reach our objectives. This chapter aims to assist students on how to build resilientness in the face of defeat, as an essential element of mastering the ability to think critically.

Resilience refers to the capacity to overcome challenges or setbacks. It is a trait that is able to be developed and cultivated with time. The most important aspect to build resilience is to recognize that failure does not mean an ending point, but the chance to learn. Through redefining mistakes as learning opportunities Students can develop the mindset of growth that allows them to see failures as steps towards improvements rather than as indicators of their own shortcomings.

One of the most important aspects to develop the ability to overcome failure is accepting it as a normal and integral element of learning. A lot of successful individuals have faced many failures before they achieved their goals. It is because of these mistakes which they've gained important insight and sharpened their thinking abilities. When they view failure as opportunities to sharpen and increase their capabilities Students can tackle the challenges with determination and persistence.

Furthermore, building resilience requires developing self-compassion and resilience situations of defeat. It is crucial for students to show compassion to themselves and to practice self-care in difficult moments. When they acknowledge their accomplishments in progress, their strengths, and achievements regardless of setbacks, they are able to remain optimistic and strive to achieve their goals.

In the end, getting help from those around you is vital to creating resilient. Students shouldn't be afraid in reaching out to their teachers and mentors as well as peers to seek advice and support. Collaboration with other students can offer new perspectives, ideas as well as strategies to overcome challenges. In addition, making connections to like-minded people helps to build a network of support that helps students remain determined and resilient when faced with the possibility of failure.

Chapter 8: Critical Thinking

In an era of a plethora of data, and where information is widely available, and sometimes conflicting, the ability to consider the implications of your thoughts has become increasingly important more than ever. Critical thinking isn't only an art, it is a mental state that allows people to analyze and analyze information in a thoughtful manner and make informed decisions and tackle problems with clearness and objectiveness.

Critical thinking is a disciplined and objective evaluation of data as well as evidence and arguments in order to formulate well-founded judgments and to make sound decisions . In the simplest sense the concept of critical thinking is challenging assumptions, acknowledging certain biases and rethinking beliefs to come to sensible conclusions. Critical thinking goes beyond accept information on its face and forces us to consider diverse perspectives, look at other perspectives and weigh the advantages and disadvantages of different arguments.

When you develop critical thinking skills Individuals are able to differentiate between credible sources of information as opposed to false and are less prone to the influence of propaganda and manipulation. Furthermore, critical thinking fosters creative thinking, intellectual curiosity and problem-solving skills, which allow people to address complex problems more clearly and with greater accuracy. Critical thinking is a crucial ability in educational settings as well as in professional settings and every day life. It creates well-rounded people who are able to make informed choices, and contributing to the society.

The elements of Critical Thinking

Critical thinking involves a variety of interconnected parts that collaborate to improve our cognitive capabilities and our decision-making abilities.

The primary part is the analysis process, in which critical thinkers take the time to analyze complex facts such as arguments or scenarios into a smaller amount to grasp the structure of their arguments and what they mean. Analyzing evidence, determining logic flaws and the credibility of sources, analysis provides the base to make informed decisions.

A second aspect is evaluating, which involves checking the credibility and validity of arguments and information. Critical thinkers assess the strengths and weaknesses of various perspectives, taking into account the evidence, context and possible biases. Through this process, they are able to differentiate between well-supported assertions as well as unsubstantiated assertions. This leads to more dependable conclusion.

Skepticism is another essential aspect in critical thought. Critical thinkers take information with a the benefit of a dose of uncertainty, examining beliefs and examining proof to back up or refute the claims. It is a way to guard against taking the information as factual which reduces the possibility of becoming a victim of misinformation or manipulative.

Problem-solving is an extension of the process of critical thinking. Through analyzing problems from multiple perspectives and evaluating various possible ways to solve them, critical thinkers arrive to innovative and successful solutions to problems. They're willing to explore new approaches and taking ideas from different disciplines. This helps them develop creative ways of solving problems.

The ability to be open-minded is an essential characteristic for critical thinking. Critical thinkers are open to new perspectives, and recognize that the beliefs they hold may be affected by biases or limitations. The acceptance of diverse perspectives allows for the development of one's intellect, increasing knowledge of complicated issues, and stimulating constructive dialog.

In the end, effective communication is the most important aspect in critical thought. The ability to communicate concepts as well as arguments in a clear and compelling manner assists in sharing ideas with other people and participating in lively conversations. In order to improve their communication abilities Critical thinkers are able to express their thoughts in a clear and concise manner, helping to facilitate informed and productive discussion.

To conclude, the elements of critical thinking have integrated skills and mental attitudes which allow individuals to think about concepts and information with precision curiosity, openness, and scepticism. Being able to think critically as well as evaluate and resolve problems with a critical, curious mindset is essential to make informed decisions and efficient communication. The importance of focusing on and developing these skills are essential in creating the development of a community that is thoughtful intelligent, sharp, and skilled people.

Overcoming Cognitive Biases

What does it mean?

It's a vital component of developing your critical thinking skills and making the right choices. Cognitive biases are innate cognitive shortcuts and patterns of thinking that result in systematic blunders when it comes to reasoning and judgement. A common bias is the confirmation bias. People prefer to look for, understand and choose information that supports their current convictions, while disregarding or rejecting evidence that is contrary to their beliefs. In order to overcome this bias it is crucial to look for different perspectives and research, which will lead to an unbiased and balanced assessment of data.

A third common bias is the availability heuristic that makes people rely on the most readily accessible information or examples which come into their minds easily in making decisions. This can hinder our knowledge of the complexity of problems and hinder our decision making. To combat the heuristic bias critics should be engaged in thoughtful research and take into consideration a wider range of information and experience. Furthermore, the anchoring bias can cause people to attribute excessive importance to the very initial information that they are exposed to and can result in biased judgements. When they recognize this bias, critical thinkers are able to consciously challenge the assumptions they have made and seek greater independence and objective evaluations.

Furthermore, the effect of bandwagon and the urge to take on a certain attitude or belief due to the fact that many people do it and can result in the herd mentality, and acceptance without scrutiny of opinions that are popular. To counter this tendency, individuals must reflect on the values they hold dear as well as independently examine evidence and resist the temptation to submit to the pressure of society without adequate examination.

Additionally, biases based on emotions, for example, the affect heuristic that is the result of letting emotions cloud judgements and can affect making decisions. In order to counter the effects of emotional biases, you must acknowledge the emotional reaction and conducting a sensible and objective evaluation of data.

Removing cognitive biases isn't an easy feat, since they are often operated subconsciously. Yet, being aware of them, reflecting on their actions and an effort to cultivate being humble in your thinking can help in reducing their impact. Involving yourself in critical thinking like pursuing different viewpoints, challenging assumptions as well as utilizing systematic analysis can help build resilience to cognitive biases. Through recognizing and confronting the underlying biases that are present, people can increase their mental capacity and make better informed well-informed, rational, and trustworthy choices in all aspects of their lives.

A key strategy for overcoming cognitive biases is by creating an environment of constructive feedback and criticism. Inviting open debate and allowing diverse perspectives can help challenge the established biases and encourage a more rational and objective way of making decisions. Through embracing different perspectives and constructive dissent, participants will gain a better comprehension of complicated issues and spot possible problems.

Uses of Overcoming Cognitive Biases:

Improves critical thinking abilities To overcome cognitive biases, you must develop analysis, and enables the growth of strong ability to think critically.

Reduces the risk of misinformation By overcoming biases, you can assist to distinguish trustworthy data from inaccurate or misleading material.

Improves problem-solving skills: Eliminating mental biases allows people to tackle problems with an open and insightful mind. .

REMEMBER

Cognitive biases are a powerful set of mental tendencies that lead individuals to make uninformed and incorrect decisions, sometimes not even noticing it. These biases are able to trick and fool people which makes them susceptible to being misled or deceived. Below are a few methods that cognitive biases are used to manipulate and deceive individuals:

1. Confirmation Bias: Human beings are inclined to search for evidence that affirms the beliefs they already have and disregard or ignore evidence that is contrary to the beliefs they hold. People can exploit this bias to present facts that are in accordance with their target's views which reinforces their beliefs and hindering them from considering other views.

2. Availability Heuristics: This bias leads people to trust data readily available instead of seeking greater understanding. The manipulators have the ability to control the nature of information and present restricted or inaccurate information in order in order to alter perceptions and take choices in their favor.

3. Anchoring Bias: Most people have a tendency to rely on the first source of information that they are presented with in making decisions. People can exploit this bias to provide an initial point of reference that can influence the recipient's perception of future information and decisions.

4. "Bandwagon Effect": urge to take on a certain belief or behavior just because other people do it is a trap for manipulators who make up an impression of a widespread consensus or popularity to influence the decisions of individuals.

5. Framing Effect: How the information is presented could influence how we consider

and judge the information. The manipulators of information can frame the data with a bias which leads people to draw certain conclusions which serve the agenda of the manipulator.

6. The Overconfidence Bias: Individuals often underestimate their skills as well as their knowledge. This can cause them to be more vulnerable to being manipulated. By exploiting this tendency, manipulators can appear as expert or authority figures, earning confidence and trust.

7. Sunk Cost Error: The desire to keep making decisions or a plan based upon past decisions, even when they're non-rational, can be used to keep people into situations that they ought to leave.

Chapter 9: Developing Intellectual Humility

It is a vital element of personal development and creating a positive dialogue. It is the ability to acknowledge the limits of our knowledge, accept that one's opinions may be faulty, and to accept different perspectives as well as new knowledge. It is about embracing an attitude which values the opportunity to learn from other people regardless of knowledge or experience, and open to feedback and constructive critique. To cultivate humility in the mind, it requires an awareness of oneself that allows individuals to openly evaluate their own weaknesses as well as their prejudices and limits.

One of the most important aspects to develop intellectual humility is acknowledging the enormous amount of human knowledge and recognizing that no individual has the complete knowledge. Adopting this mindset can lead to a more humble and open way of thinking about one's beliefs and thoughts, thereby creating a healthy foundation for growth and learning.

It also requires actively looking for different perspectives, and being open to the opinions of others in a genuine interest. Engaging in a an empathetic and respectful manner

Conversations allow people to broaden the scope of their knowledge by challenging preconceived notions as well as expanding their mind perspectives. In addition, being open constructive feedback and criticism can help develop the ability to be humble in your thinking. Instead of viewing criticism as an attack on oneself people who are humble see it as an opportunity to gain knowledge and improve. When they are humble enough to acknowledge their mistakes and gaining knowledge from their mistakes, they are able to improve their understanding and enhance their decision-making process.

In addition, a greater sense of an attitude of intellectual humility is beneficial in resolving conflict and encouraging healthy interpersonal relationships. If you approach disputes with the ability to be open and able to understand other peoples views, one will create a more open and a more collaborative atmosphere.

Education is a crucial factor in cultivating intellectual humour. Teachers can stress the importance of questioning beliefs, making students think critically about knowledge and willing to accept the possibility of being incorrect. Instilling a culture in the classroom which values curiosity, open discussion and sharing of different perspectives can assist in developing intellectual humility at beginning at an early time.

I will now make sure your aware of its significance using Real Life examples:

Learning and accepting constructive criticism. A student receiving feedback about the essay by either a teacher or another peer and truly takes the advice to heart and makes changes in order to improve their work shows intellectual aplomb.

Changes in political views with new data One who will be willing to reconsider their beliefs about politics after conducting research and considering different perspectives shows an intellectual confidence.

The teachers who emphasize the teaching of students to challenge the assumptions of others, analyze information and look at different perspectives, encourage academic humility in the classroom.

Discussions that are open and tolerant two people who have opposing faiths and beliefs, who are engaged in dialogue that is respectful and open to others and seek to learn from their perspectives and show an intellectual humbleness.

Being open to different views on social issues. Community members who take part in an open discussion about an issue that is sensitive, and paying attention to the various perspectives without becoming defensive, shows the intellectual dignity.

Engaging students in inquiry-based learning: Schools that use inquiry-based learning techniques, in which students can freely explore their interests and ask questions as well as encourage intellectual humility and self-reliance.

The real-world examples show the depth of intellectual

It can be seen in many situations, from education and personal growth to interactions with others

and process of decision-making. Accepting humility in the process of decision-making allows people to open their minds, become more compassionate, and eager to continue learning, which ultimately contributes to a more tolerant and more harmonious society .

The Art of Asking Question

Asking questions is at the core to critical thinking efficient communications, and a meaningful education. The power of questions is for gathering information, induce interest, and stimulate an enlightened analysis. Learning to ask questions is being able to ask questions which are simple as well as open in the context. Questions that are open-ended, for instance stimulate deeper thought and prompt deeper responses. This allows individuals to look deeper into complicated issues and think from multiple angles.

Also, it requires the use of active listening and empathy. When they pay attention to their replies, people may follow up with a series of questions to delve into the topic. This shows an interest in the subject but also allows to gain a deeper understanding of the subject and people's point of view. Engaging in questions that are genuinely asked creates an open and non-judgmental atmosphere that encourages open dialogue and strengthening connections with other people.

In addition, they can serve as useful tools in problem solving and making decisions. In the face of challenges by asking the right questions, it will help to identify the root cause as well as explore solutions and determine the possible results. This also allows for a more collaborative method, where teams are able to think about and tackle issues together using their various perspectives

Perspectives and abilities.

When it comes to education, the art of asking questions is crucial to making students active with the process of learning. Teachers who are skilled use questions that provoke thought to spark discussions, foster critical thinking and assist students in learning to learn on their own. Through asking questions that demand the application and analysis of ideas to develop a greater understanding of the subject and a lasting memory of the information.

But, mastering the technique of asking questions demands humility and willingness to acknowledge that one does not have the complete answer. Sometimes, the best approach can be "I don't know, but I'm curious to find out." This creates a culture of ongoing learning. It encourages everyone especially leaders and experts to be open to new information and concepts.

IT'S IMPORTANCE

Acquiring Knowledge : Asking questions helps us seek*

Information and knowledge gained on the vast array of subjects that allow us to broaden our perspective on the world.

By asking the use of questions, we will get clarifications and increase understanding of complicated ideas, making sure that we are aware of the topic.

"Problem Solving: Asking correct questions can lead to pinpointing the root of the problem helping to solve problems effectively and making decisions.

Critical Thinking: Questions stimulate critical thinking, by forcing us to look at assumptions, examine evidence and consider different perspectives prior to coming to conclusions.

Establishing relationships Inquiring questions creates interesting conversations, increases relationships with other people and shows genuine interest in the thoughts and experience of others.

"Empathy and Understanding" The ability to ask thoughtful questions allows us to be aware of others' perspectives feelings, experiences, and emotions encouraging empathy and understanding communicating.

Adaptability and learning Affirming an open-minded attitude through asking questions allows for continuous learning and apprehension, especially in a constantly changing globe.

Conflict resolution: Having questions during conflicts may assist in uncovering the root causes that can facilitate communication and can lead to positive and mutually beneficial solutions.

Inspiring Innovation: The questions encourage creativity and ingenuity and encourage us to think about different ideas and question traditional thinking.

Self-Reflection: Asking ourselves introspective questions helps us become aware of ourselves and encourages individual growth. It allows us to see areas of improvements and establish meaningful goals.

Gaining Perspectives: By asking questions that offer a variety of perspectives that challenge our thinking, we expand our perspective and open ourselves to new perspectives.

Chapter 10: Analyzing Arguments And Evidence

Examining arguments and supporting arguments is an important element of critical thinking. It lets people make educated judgements and reach solid conclusion. When confronted with arguments either in writing verbal or written, or another medium Analyzing an argument requires analyzing the logic, structure as well as supporting evidence. The critical thinker evaluates the validity and coherence of the argument by identifying the flaws and weaknesses which could undermine its legitimacy.

To analyze arguments, the very first process is to pinpoint the primary claim or argument made by the writer or speaker. The understanding of the primary point assists to understand the context of the statements as well as the evidence presented. Critical thinkers will then assess the credibility of the arguments that is presented to back up the assertion. This could include analyzing the reliability and quality of the sources used and determining if the information comes from empirical evidence or is merely anecdotal. making sure that the evidence is valid and enough to justify the assertion.

Additionally, the process of analyzing arguments involves finding and evaluating any logical errors that are that are present. The fallacies can be characterized as errors of reasoning which could lead to faulty or misleading arguments. Examples of fallacies include ad hominem attacks where arguments are attacked attacking the person who made it, not the argument's substance, as well as sweeping generalizations where the generalizations are based on only a small amount of evidence. Being aware of fallacies makes it easier for critical thinkers to recognize weak or misleading arguments, and to avoid being deceived with deceitful rhetoric.In aside from analyzing the specific arguments, it's important to look at the larger circumstances in the way they are presented. Consider any prejudices, hidden agendas or personal interests that might impact the argument's structure and delivery. Critical thinkers are also looking at opposing arguments and counter-arguments and are constantly seeking out alternative viewpoints in order to get a greater comprehension of the problem.

When it comes to the analysis of evidence the critical thinker employs the combination of skeptical thinking and an open mind. They evaluate evidence sources for quality, accuracy as well as credibility. They take into consideration aspects such as expert knowledge of the author, popularity of the journal, and also the methods used to gather information. They are flexible to any possibility of new information could alter or challenge their original beliefs, which is a sign of the humility of their minds.

In gaining proficiency in studying evidence and argument people become proficient in discerning between legitimate and false arguments, leading to rounded and sophisticated decision making. For academic institutions it is essential to evaluate research studies and coming to well-substantiated conclusions. It helps people navigate the ever-changing stream of data in a sensitive and critical manner and enables people to make well-informed decisions and participate in constructive discussions and discussions. In the end, analysing arguments and data empowers people to be more adept and better prepared to critically engage with the world they live in.

Merits of Analyzing Arguments and Evidence:

Information-based Decision Making: By analysing evidence and arguments, one are able to make informed decisions that are based on solid knowledge and reasoning.

Effective Problem-Solving A capacity to analyze data allows for better solving problems as people can determine reliable and relevant solution.

Beware of false information by analyzing arguments can help in identifying false or misleading facts, and minimizing the chance of being deceived by false statements.

Enhancing communication: People who understand arguments are able to communicate their opinions more convincingly, and take part with more constructively in conversations.

Intellectual Empowerment: Analyzing the evidence can help to empower your mind by encouraging the ability to think independently and critically.

An example from real life: A person reviewing a product online employs an analysis of critical quality to differentiate real reviews and false ones, and make an educated decision on purchasing the item.

Improved Academic Performance: Students that examine arguments and research critically succeed in academic situations with well-written and logical tasks.

The promotion of Scientific Inquiry: Analyzing evidence is a crucial aspect of scientific research. This ensures that findings are trustworthy and can be trusted.

Demerits of Analyzing Arguments and Evidence:

Time-consuming: Analyzing arguments or the evidence in a thorough manner can take time especially when you are dealing in the presence of complex or lengthy information.

Cognitive Load: The act of critical analysis is physically demanding, particularly in the face of a large number of contradicting information.

Beliefs and biases: Even while analyzing arguments, a person might inadvertently allow their personal prejudgments and biases affect their judgments.

An example from real life: during the course of a debate on politics viewers may be able to analyze the arguments of both candidates, however, they may not be consciously focusing on data that is in accordance to their personal political beliefs.

Hidden Nuances: When in an effort to evaluate data, it is possible to overlook tiny details that may be significant to the final evaluation.

The polarization of analysis: A skeptic's view can result in an irrational view, in which the people are skeptical of all sources and hinders constructive dialog.

An example from real life: Someone who is exposed to a variety of conspiracies may be so incredulous of any information they dismiss credible information that comes from reliable sources.

Information Overload: In this modern age of information, an plethora of information may overwhelm people and make it difficult to properly evaluate arguments and the evidence.

Analyzing evidence and arguments has many advantages, such as an informed approach to decision-making, efficient problem solving and avoiding misinformation. It also has its own drawbacks, including time consumption as well as cognitive burden and the potential for bias. However, the advantages from developing this capability outweigh its drawbacks because it allows people to deal with a difficult environment with clarity, awareness, and more discernible method of processing information.

Chapter 11: Decision Making And Uncertainty

The process of making decisions is a fundamental aspect of our everyday lives that determines our choices as well as our outcomes and paths. But, the decision-making process is frequently ensnared with uncertainty as we face a lack of data, uncertain variables and uncertain outcomes. The chapter focuses on the challenges of making decisions under uncertain outcomes, examining the processes of cognitive thinking required, the issues presented, as well as strategies for making informed choices in the face of lack of data.

1. Understanding Decision Making:

It is a thought-based method that requires choosing the best course of action, or deciding between various options. It's an integral part of our lives, taking place throughout a range of situations including personal and workplace settings. A successful decision-making process involves critical thinking, problem-solving abilities, and the capacity to assess the likely consequences of every option.

2. The Role of Uncertainty:

In the process of the process of making decisions, since it results when pertinent information is missing, insufficient or unclear. Inability to anticipate the future with confidence may cause anxiety and even trepidation which makes making decisions an extremely difficult task. But, understanding and managing the uncertainty is essential to make solid and well-informed decision.

3. Types of Uncertainty:

The risk uncertainty form of uncertainty refers to situations in which the odds of different outcomes are established. Decision makers are able to make use of tools like probabilities and statistics to analyze and mitigate risks.

Ambiguity occurs in the absence of clarity or knowledge regarding the likely consequences.

In uncertain situations there is a chance that decision makers have little information from which to make a decision.

Inattention: It occurs in situations where decision makers aren't aware of crucial information or possible effects, which makes it challenging to evaluate the risk accurately.

4. The Challenge of Uncertainty in Decision Making

In order to reduce the risk of uncertainty, managers should gather accurate and pertinent information from a variety of sources. Complete data collection can make up for any gaps and give the most accurate information about the present.

Asking for Expert Opinions: expert opinions from specialists in your field could provide useful insights and viewpoints, particularly in the case of complex or unfamiliar scenarios.

Scenario Planning: Thinking about various possibilities of scenarios and the potential outcome allows decision makers plan for various scenarios and reduce the effects of uncertainties.

Evaluation of Risk and mitigation The identification of potential risks that are associated with every option, and establishing mitigation strategies is a great way to in reducing uncertainty.

Models and Decision Trees Making use of decision trees or mathematical models may aid in making sense of probabilities, and in determining the most effective strategy based upon existing data.

Acceptance of Uncertainty: Recognizing the fact that uncertainty is inevitable, and getting confident in the face of uncertainty can lead to greater confidence in decision-making.

5. Uses of Decision Making and Uncertainty:

Business Management: in business the importance of decision-making is to the strategic plan of action, allocation of resources markets analysis, managing risk.

Financial Planning: Individuals employ the process of decision-making to distribute their funds efficiently, invest investments and plan their retirement.

Diagnostics for Medical Conditions: In the field of the field of healthcare, making a decision is crucial in order to make a correct diagnosis, treatment selection and the care of patients.

Public Policy: Decision-making influences the public policy, legislative action and government initiatives that solve societal problems.

Educational Choices: Students have to make the decisions about their academic path as well as their course choices, along with the planning of their careers.

Personal Relationships: Decision-making is a key element in interpersonal relationships, including choosing partners, to the resolution of disputes.

Problem Solving

The ability to solve problems is essential that allows people to face obstacles, take effective choices, and reach the goals they set. If it is paired with critical thinking, problem-solving is a great tool for thinking through complex issues, developing new solutions, and allowing sensible choices. This chapter examines the interaction between problem-solving and critical thinking. The chapter focuses on how integrating the two cognitive systems results in more effective and productive problem-solving results.

With the help of critical analysis, they are able to gather and evaluate pertinent evidence using the latest research and data as well as professional insights to help inform their approach to problem solving. The evidence-based method assists to identify patterns, trends and possible solutions, while simultaneously reducing the effect of preconceived ideas and biases. Additionally, critical thinking stimulates the ability to think creatively when solving problems by encouraging people to look for new and innovative strategies. In challenging the conventional approach and accepting a variety of perspectives Critical thinking allows people to come up with innovative solutions and ideas for solving complicated issues.

After a variety of possible possibilities are identified and analyzed, critical thinking plays an important role in evaluating and choosing the most suitable option. With careful consideration of benefits of each option, their drawbacks and possible effects, one can take an informed decision that is in line with their objectives and beliefs. It also allows people to identify potential risks, forecast outcomes and anticipate challenges that could arise which can lead to an enlightened approach to problem solving.

Once solutions are in place the critical mind remains in place as it allows people to keep track of developments, modify strategies as required, and participate with continuous development. Thinking critically plays an important part in refining the problem-solving abilities and allowing individuals to learn conclusions from previous experiences and use those lessons for future problems.

After the issue is identified the critical mind guides people to analyze and gather relevant evidence. This involves doing studies, gathering data in consultation with experts, as well as taking into consideration different perspectives in order to get an comprehension of the complexity of the issue. Critical thinkers are skilled at checking the validity and reliability of their evidence, and avoid any pitfalls caused by inaccurate information or inaccurate sources. Analytical thinking ensures the decision making process is built on solid accurate information and trustworthy data.

When you are able to grasp the issues and facts at the ready, critical thinking can unleash imagination in the creation of possible solutions. Ideation sessions, brainstorming along with exercises in lateral thinking help to generate new thinking.

Critical thinkers look for new ways to approach problems that challenge conventional thinking, as well as accept differing perspectives, expanding the possibilities for options and enhancing the chances of discovering innovative and efficient solutions.

Critical thinking is then brought in to help with the evaluation and choice of options. This involves constantly evaluating every possible solution's strengths and weaknesses while considering its viability, effectiveness and ethical implications. When weighing these elements critically, they can make educated choices, deciding on the appropriate option which is compatible with the overall intentions and beliefs of the particular situation.

Implementation is a process that requires continuous analysis and critical thinking. It involves developing plans for action as well as monitoring progress and adjusting strategies as needed. Critical thinkers stay alert and stay on top of any potential challenges or obstacles and making adjustments based on data to ensure that the plan is carried out successfully. of the plan.

In the process of problem solving the critical mind encourages reflection thinking as well as continuous learning. People analyze the results of their choices, and reflect on their successes and mistakes to gain valuable insight that can be applied to future endeavors. Self-awareness helps to grow personally which allows people to develop their thinking skills and methods constantly.

The conclusion is that problem-solving using critical thinking is a continuous and integrating cognitive method that enables people to tackle issues with clarity, creativity and a strategic approach. Through the combination of problem-solving as well as evidence analysis, innovative ideas, critical decision-making and reflection Critical thinking is the basis for successful and long-lasting solutions. By embracing this holistic approach to problem solving allows people to face complex challenges by demonstrating confidence, strength and the flexibility needed to succeed in a constantly changing globalized.

Chapter 12: Critical Thinking In Media And Information Literacy

Critical thinking plays an integral part in the process of media and information literacy. It gives people an understanding of how to navigate the huge and varied array of information available today's digital world. In a world in which information is abounding however, it is not always trustworthy. critical thinking is an effective shield against false information or biases as well as propaganda. Media literacy and information literacy require the capacity to judge the reliability and credibility of the sources used, analyze actual biases that are at the root, and differentiate between authentic information and sensationalized information. Critical thinkers are knowledgeable consumers of information and analytically skilled to challenge, validate and verify information prior to taking it for what it is.

Critical thinking allows people to discern the motivations behind these messages by recognizing convincing techniques and subtle motives. The ability to analyze media content with a keen eye allows people to recognize potential biases, stereotypes as well as misinformation that could be incorporated into the story. Furthermore, critical thinking allows users to actively engage with the content and encourages discussion and constructive dialogs instead of passive acceptance.

When it comes to information literacy, critical thinking is crucial to evaluate the reliability and quality of information sources. With the abundance of information on the web It is essential to differentiate between reliable sources from those that are not. The critical thinker will verify the writer's qualifications, evaluate the publication's credibility, and evaluate the accuracy and timeliness of information. Through this process, the individuals take informed choices based on reliable and reliable information.

Additionally, critical thinking encourages the ability to be open-minded towards diverse opinions and views. Instead of settling for echo chambers and prejudices, the media and knowledgeable individuals are constantly seeking different perspectives, and recognize the value of being exposed to diverse opinions in order to gain an in-depth understanding of complicated questions.

Teachers play an important part in encouraging the critical thought process in media and information literacy. Incorporating critical thinking exercises as well as fact-checking exercises, discussions around media ethics within the curriculum for education, teachers are able to provide students with the knowledge required to navigate the online world in a responsible manner.

To conclude, critical thinking is an integral part of information literacy and media. Through the development of analytical and critical thought, thinking critically enables people to make sense of the information age in a more thoughtful manner. People with the ability to think critically can make educated decisions, interact with media critically and help build a more informed and a democratic society. Insisting on critical thinking within education and media initiatives is crucial to fostering an intelligent and responsible citizen.

Believing in what you read on the internet is the most fundamental use that requires critical analysis. The following are reasons critical thinking is vital when assessing media content:

The potential for bias and agendas Potential Bias and Agenda: Media outlets could be awash with bias and agendas.

certain biases, agendas, or motives that could influence how they convey particular information. Thinking critically can help us recognize potential biases, and then take a look at alternative perspectives.

Fake news and misinformation In this digital age the spread of fake news and false information are easily spread through social media, as well as on other media platforms. Critical thinking allows us to examine the credibility and sources of the information we are given before taking it for granted.

Incontextual A lot of media stories are presented with a simplified form without the contextual context to gain a full comprehension. The critical thinking process prompts us to search for more information and context so that we can avoid mistakes in interpretation.

Sensationalism: The media often prioritizes stories that are sensational or in-your-face over truth and objectivity. The ability to think critically allows us to detect sensationalism, and then dig into the actual facts.

Confirmation bias: In the absence of any critical thinking skills, we might have a tendency to accept data that is consistent with our beliefs that we have already established which can reinforce the confirmation bias. Critical thinking requires the mind to question its assumptions, and look at contradictory facts.

Slightly limited information Media reports can provide just a small portion of an issue that is complex. The critical thinking process encourages us to take information from a variety of sources in order to develop an understanding that is more complete.

Propaganda and Manipulation Certain media outlets may employ manipulative techniques or use propaganda techniques in order to change the public's opinions. A critical approach helps us recognize the tactics employed and be able to make a judgment on the message they intend to send.

Lack of fact-checking Media outlets do not always verify their facts. We are compelled to investigate claims on our own before deciding to accept them as truthful.

Overreliance on headlines: Focusing only on headlines or short summaries could result in misinterpretations. Critical thinking encourages you to read more than headlines and engaging in lengthy article content.

Business Interests: Media companies could place a high value on advertising revenue or commercial interests that affect their content. The critical thinking process prompts us to look at the effects of commercial influence on the content we present.

Applying Critical Thinking to Personal Growth

The application of critical thinking to personal growth can be a transformational experience that helps individuals increase their awareness of themselves, conquer barriers, and attain significant growth. Through the use of critical thinking abilities that allow individuals to objectively evaluate their actions, attitudes and practices, challenging their assumptions, and identify areas for enhancement. The ability to reflect on self is an essential part of personal growth because critical thinkers evaluate their motivations, values, and objectives, making sure they reflect their true personas.

Critical thinking can also allow individuals to look back at their past and errors, gaining valuable insights and insight. Instead of avoiding mistakes or justifying shortcomings Critical thinkers face challenges with a critical mindset looking for opportunities for learning and improvement. This method helps build resilience as well as a positive outlook and encourages people to accept difficulties and consider them steps towards personal growth.

Additionally, critical thinking assists in establishing real and lasting objectives. Through evaluating their strengths, weaknesses and assets, individuals are able to be well informed about the areas they would like to develop and the strategies required to achieve their goals. A thoughtful plan ensures your personal growth goals can be targeted and tailored to the individual's goals.

Applying critical thinking to your personal development also requires seeking out diverse views and providing constructive feedback. The most critical thinkers seek out input from peers, mentors as well as loved ones, and consider different perspectives as opportunities to development. When they are open to feedback, people are able to identify weaknesses and other areas that could require more attention. This encourages continual personal improvement.

Critical thinking also promotes the development of an intellectual mindset and acknowledges that personal growth is a continual process, with no set end date. Instead of asserting that they have all the solutions, critical thinkers accept the uncertainty of life, being open to fresh information and inviting possibilities for self-discovery as well as improvement.

Additionally the application of critical thinking to your personal development requires a thorough assessment of previous experiences as well as mistakes. Instead of dwelling upon failures and dismissing them as merely mistakes, critical thinkers tackle the challenges they face by pursuing curiosity and the desire to gain knowledge. They examine the causes which led to specific outcomes they identify the patterns that led to them and identify important lessons to guide any future decisions.

The use of critical thinking in personal development extends to the setting of goals that aren't just high-minded, but also practical and beneficial. Critical thinkers take a close look at their ambitions and match them with their goals and values. They can break larger goals into smaller, manageable tasks, and develop an outline that is feasible and long-lasting. Through the use of critical thinking when planning goals, one are able to focus their efforts on growth areas that truly connect with their true self, creating an inner sense of purpose as well as an intrinsic drive.

Additionally, critical thinkers look for diverse viewpoints and positive input from reliable sources. They are grateful for the advice of their mentors, friends and family members, knowing that their insights from other people can illuminate aspects they may overlook. Being open to opinions and feedback is a great way to enrich your personal development journey by increasing critical thinkers' knowledge of themselves, and helping them make focused improvement.

The final conclusion is that applying an approach to self-development can be a self-empowering and dynamic method. It takes self-awareness, reflection and the ability to learn and question from the failures as well as successes. When they develop critical thinking skills for individual development, people can begin a path to continuous improvement that is genuine, purposeful and in alignment to their ideals and beliefs. Utilizing critical thinking to personal growth can help build resilience, adaptability and an enlightened mindset which ultimately leads to a more happy and fulfilling living.

Chapter 13: Decoding Complexity In Politics

Let's expose the reality of the Leaders and System

Voting based on emotions If they don't think critically, voters can be convinced by the appeals of their emotions charismatic individuals, empty promises, instead of taking a look at a candidate's qualifications policy, the track record.

Inattention to Facts and Evidence Individuals who do not have ability to think critically may overlook or ignore significant facts and evidence concerning an individual's background, or about policies, resulting in uninformed choices.

Not recognizing the power of propaganda and misinformation: Candidates or their supporters could exploit absence of critical thinking disseminating misinformation or engaging in manipulative propagandists, which can lead users to base their decisions upon false or inaccurate facts.

The following Populist leaders: Populist leaders often appeal to their emotions and stoke grievances. This is particularly appealing for those who do not possess analytical skills. The result is being elected by those who place short-term popularity over the stability of long-term administration.

Partisan Loyalty: With no the ability to think critically, people may simply adhere to the ideology or party's position without weighing the possible effects or examining other viewpoints.

Ineffective Policy: Leaders chosen by the voters who lack the ability to make rational decisions may be able to implement actions that are not most beneficial for the citizens of this country that can result in inefficiency and adverse outcomes.

Inability to hold leaders accountable: Critical thinking helps individuals to demand accountability from their leaders to their actions and choices. In the absence of it, individuals may be able to overlook or justify the poor performance of their leaders, resulting in an absence of accountability.

Polarization and division: Insufficient critical thinking could result in political polarization because people can become ensconced in their opinions without searching for an agreement or grasping opposing opinions.

The erosion of Democracy People who lack the ability to critically think is more vulnerable to the deterioration of democratic principles, since they might not be able to see the dangers to democracy and its institutions and procedures.

Lower Civic Engagement people who lack critical thinking abilities could become disconnected from politics, leading to less participation in the voting process as well as a decrease in civic involvement.

The absence of critical thinking abilities when the selection and follow-up of a leadership can result in uninformed decision-making, vulnerability to manipulation and possibly negative consequences for the society. Inspiring and promoting critical thinking is essential to developing an informed and engaged electorate that can make well-considered choices in the political arena.

The phenomenon of people who are not educated choosing their leaders on the basis of religious beliefs is commonplace in some communities. This underscores the necessity to encourage and promote thoughtfulness in the voting procedure. We will explore this topic further:

Emotional Appeal and Identity Politics: Uneducated*

people who lack exposure to different perspectives or discerning analyses, are more prone to appeals to emotions as well as identity-based political issues. Some candidates may make use of religious symbols or associations in order to appeal to the voters' feelings, causing people to vote in accordance with their religious beliefs instead of substantive policies.

The Risks of Manipulation If they lack critical thinking abilities uninformed voters could be manipulated through politicians who profit from the religious beliefs of their constituents to gain advantage. Religious rhetoric can be used by leaders to deflect attention from more important issues of policy or create tensions within the populace.

Inadequacy of Policy Evaluation A voter who is not educated may be unable to grasp complex proposals for policy or might not be able to prioritize analysis when making a decision. Instead, they might depend on their religious beliefs to provide a simple and quick method of deciding on a potential candidate.

Impact on Democracy Based solely on religion during voting can cause the formation of groups that vote based on religion, disenfranchising minority groups, and thereby compromising the fundamentals of a plural and open democracy.

Not focusing on qualifications and competence Prioritizing religion over the candidate's skills and education, uninformed voters could inadvertently choose those who aren't equipped as well as experience required for successful management.

Distracting attention away from the real Problems: focusing on religion or identities rather than on policy suggestions could divert attention away from important questions like economic development or social welfare Governance, which can hinder advancement on crucial issues.

Promoting the polarization of society: relying solely on religious vote can cause the society becoming divided by allowing voters to align along the religious inclinations instead of being open to dialogue and finding an agreement.

Reduced accountability: When the leaders elected are primarily by their religious affiliation and beliefs, they could assume that their positions are secure, and therefore less accountable to their voters and this can result in the administration that is not geared towards the general well-being of the country.

3. Learning to deal with complex issues: The development of analytical skills allows citizens to consider difficult policy issues and to grasp the implications various proposals that go beyond religious affiliations.

4. A focus on inclusion The process of critical thinking promotes the notion of inclusiveness and helps voters consider the rights of everyone regardless of religion.

5. Encouragement of Dialogue: Stressing an open mind can foster positive dialogue among the voters and encourage voters to engage in discussions about policy issues instead of relying on polarizing religion-based identity.

6. Transparency and Accountability the public puts policy priorities ahead of religion, the leaders could be more accountable to their performance and decisions.

To conclude, encouraging the ability to think critically is crucial when it comes to voting processes in which voters with no education might rely on their religious beliefs to cast their votes. The idea of encouraging voters to judge potential candidates according to the policies, qualifications, as well as the ability to govern fosters an educated, diverse and accountable democratic process.

The Role of Critical Thinking:

The promotion of critical thinking is crucial for addressing these problems:

1. A Critical and Objective Evaluation of Policy: This invites the public to judge candidates on their policies, skills as well as their ability to tackle the challenges of society, rather than on their religion.

2. Fact-checking and verification The power of critical thinking can prompt people to verify the facts presented by the candidates, making sure that their choices are based on reliable and accurate data.

Chapter 14: The Concept Of Critical Thinking

Critical thinking refers to a attitude and skill that allows people to analyse the meaning, evaluation, and interpretation of data in a rational and organized way. It requires actively and skillfully understanding, applying, and analyzing the synesizing and evaluation of the information from different sources to formulate well-balanced judgements and take informed choices.

Today, critical thinking is becoming more important because of a variety of reasons:

1. Information overload Information Overload: We live in an age with unprecedented access to information thanks to the internet and other digital platforms. But this volume of information poses the task of separating accurate pertinent, trustworthy, and accurate facts from false information, biased or a superficial view. Critical thinking helps individuals traverse this sea of information through evaluating credibility,

confirming the authenticity of sources, and in identifying logic errors.

2. The spread of fake news and misinformation The proliferation of false news and misleading information is now a serious issue within our world. Critical thinking gives people the ability to evaluate critically informational articles and social media content and other online media that allow them to distinguish facts from fiction, and then form well-informed judgements. It can help combat the negative consequences of false information in public debate, decision-making as well as democratic processes.

3. The art of solving complex problems: Contemporary issues, whether personal or professional, tend to be complicated and diverse. The ability to think critically allows individuals to divide complex problems into manageable pieces, look at multiple perspectives, analyze evidence, and develop new strategies. It promotes innovation,

flexibility and adaptability when it comes to problem solving methods, which allows individuals to solve problems effectively.

4. The process of making a decision is that is brimming with possibilities and options, making a decision can seem daunting. Critical thinking offers a systematic way to make decisions by weighing various factors, taking into account the evidence, considering risks and the possible consequences. The ability to make rational choices that are based on their beliefs as well as their goals and available data.

5. Citizenship and Democracy Critical thinking plays an essential role in the development of active and educated citizens. It enables people to rethink beliefs, confront biases, and participate in civil debate. In evaluating the validity of political statements and evaluating policies and analyzing the implications of their decisions, people are able to contribute to a active and a democratic society.

Critical thinking is an essential ability in today's world because of the influx in information and the apprehension of erroneous information, the complexity of issues, the necessity to be able to take effective decisions and the need for active participation in the civic life. When you develop and apply abilities to think critically, one improve their capacity to think critically as well as solve challenges and deal with concepts and information in a thoughtful, discerning approach.

The problems posed by an amount of information we have today in our digital time.

The amount of information that is available could be an overwhelming task. Since the advent of the internet and other digital platforms the internet is constantly flooded with a flow of data and news stories, as well as video updates for social media sites and much more. It can be difficult to filter through the plethora of information in order to identify what's pertinent, precise and trustworthy.

1. Accuracy and Quality There is a lack of rigorous editorial control. This leads to various degrees of quality and trustworthiness of the content that is provided. False information, false news and biased content are all over the place and make it difficult for users to differentiate reliable and authentic sources from those which are incorrect or completely incorrect.

2. Confirmation Bias Confirmation Bias: The ease of accessing online information permits individuals to search for information that supports the beliefs they already have and their biases. This bias of confirmation can create echo chambers, and restrict the ability to learn from different perspectives that hinder critical thinking, as well as the ability to develop an informed and well-rounded opinion.

3. Information Fatigue: Continuous exposure to an ever-changing amount of information

may cause mental fatigue and the fatigue of information. The mental overload resulted from the continuous requirement to process, filter and analyze information could decrease attention spans, and can hinder the ability to focus on the deepest analysis and analysis.

4. A fragmented attention: The modern world often promotes multitasking as well as scattered attention. Users frequently shift between different sources of information for example, browsing several tabs, checking for notifications, or scrolling through the feeds of social media. The constant switch-up can hinder an in-depth and focused comprehension of difficult topics.

5. Filter Bubbles and Personalization Algorithms Search engines' algorithms and social media sites often customize the information users see in accordance with their habits and choices. Although this may improve users' experience, it also results in filter bubbles where users are only presented with information that is in line with their

views, which limits the possibility of gaining a broad perspective as well as hindering the ability to think critically.

6. Information Overload and. Information gaps: Despite the fact that there's an abundance of data, there may there be large gaps in the information. Some subjects or areas do not are covered equally or have equal visibility on the internet, leading to an information imbalance and restricted access to specific kinds of information.

In order to overcome these obstacles, one must acquire the ability to think critically, which includes the evaluation of sources, fact-checking and verifying data, as well as recognizing prejudices and looking for different perspectives. It is crucial to think about the consumption of information with a critical and sceptical mindset, continuously looking at and evaluating the data you encounter. In addition, adopting methods that include setting boundaries as well as practicing mindfulness as well as seeking out reliable and trustworthy sources could help ease problems posed by an amount of information available online.

Critical thinking abilities are essential to survive the current overwhelming information as they help people to navigate through the overwhelming quantity of information, evaluate the credibility of sources, distinguish facts from opinions, identify patterns of thinking, examine complex data and overcome cognitive biases make informed choices, and actively interact in the world of information they are exposed to. Learning to develop critical thinking are essential to be informed, discerning and empowered users of information in the modern world.

Chapter 15: Understanding Information Overload

Information overload refers to the condition of being overwhelmed by large quantities of data, usually which causes difficulties with organizing, processing and understanding the data. It's caused by various factors that are prevalent in our technological age that can have diverse effects on people and society. We will explore the reasons and the effects of excessive information further:

Causes of Information Overload:

1. Technology Advancements Rapid development of technology, specifically digital media and the internet is making it more convenient than ever before to connect and share data. Access to information via various platforms and devices is a major factor in the massive amount of information.

2. Digital Platforms as well as Social Media: Social media platforms, news aggregators and websites for sharing content continuously generate huge quantities of data. It is easy to

publish and sharing content results in an exponential growth in the amount of information available.

3. 24/7 News Cycle 24/7 News Cycle: Traditional media outlets as well as websites operate round all hours of the day, offering an unending stream of stories and updates. The constant content of the news cycle creates a constant overload of information that people face as they try to keep pace with the ever-changing streams of information.

4. Information Accessibility It is easy to access data from a variety of sources as well as the ability to search for information in a short time contributes to the huge amount of information. The increased accessibility to content and distribution means that anyone is able to make information available, leading to the exponential growth of quantity of information.

Effects of Information Overload:

1. Cognitive Overload: The overload of information creates a major strain on the brain's resources and can lead to cognitive stress. The brain's ability to store and process information is often overwhelmed. which results in a decrease in concentration, recall of memories, and difficulties when it comes to focusing on work.

2. Lower Quality Decisions: Due to a plethora of information available, some people be overwhelmed by decisions, which makes difficult to take good decision-making. A myriad of choices and conflicting information could result in a lack of decision making or rash, uninformed choices.

Chapter 16: The Fundamentals Of Critical Thinking

Critic thinking is a complex cognitive activity that involves continuously and effectively conceptualizing, analysing the results of evaluating, synthesising, and utilizing information to formulate sound judgments, and to make well-informed choices. The following is a complete review of the underlying principles and the components of critical thinking

1. Clearness: The process of critical thinking stresses the significance of clearly and precisely thinking. It is the art of expressing thoughts or arguments in a succinct understanding, consistent and clear way, while avoiding vague or unclear terminology. The clarity of language ensures that the thoughts and logic are clearly communicated.

2. Accuracy: Accuracy plays a major role to thinking critically. This means striving to achieve accuracy, rigor as well as truthfulness when thinking and reasoning. Critical thinkers

are those who seek out trustworthy information, validate the sources and stay clear of errors and biases when analyzing and evaluating.

3. The art of precision in critical thinking requires the attention to detail as well as specificity. This means using precise terminology and not relying on broadening or simplifying. The use of precision helps refine thoughts, arguments and conclusion, ensuring that they're precise and nitty-gritty.

4. Relevance: The critical thinker will look at the significance of knowledge and concepts in relation to the situation or context in question. They try to find relationships between concepts, evidence and arguments in order to assess their importance and pertinence. Relevance is the way to ensure that only relevant data is considered, and non-relevant or irrelevant factors do not receive the same weightage.

5. Deep Thinking: Critical thinking is about the ability to go beyond superficial understanding

and engaging in deep research. It is about digging beneath the surface of thoughts assertions, arguments or statements in order to expose the root beliefs, biases or even logical fallacies. It requires an examination of the complexity and implications of knowledge in order to gain a deeper knowledge.

6. The ability to think in broad terms: Critical thinkers aim to expand their thinking through the consideration of multiple perspectives, different viewpoints and a range of different sources. They realize that an extensive knowledge requires an exposure to various concepts and proofs. Breadth assists in avoiding narrow-mindedness, and encourages a more comprehensive and holistic way of life.

7. Logical reasoning Logical Reasoning is an essential element in critical thought. It is the capacity to evaluate, identify and formulate valid and solid arguments. Critical thinkers utilize logic, inductive and deductive thinking logic frameworks and an analysis based on

evidence to evaluate the credibility and logic of arguments and claims.

8. The concept of fairness emphasizes honesty and fairness. It demands that you approach the world with a wide-ranging mind unaffected by personal biases and preconceptions. Critical thinkers attempt to analyze the evidence and arguments in a neutral manner by considering various perspectives, and being open to rethink their beliefs on the basis of an objective evaluation.

9. Intellectual Honesty: This is an essential tenet of critical thinking. It is about being honest and genuine in the research process, accepting the limitations of knowledge, as well as accepting self-reflection as well as critique. Critical thinkers are committed to the integrity of their thinking, recognizing errors or shortcomings in their thinking and being eager to grow and learn.

10. Critical Thinking: It is tightly linked to problem-solving. It requires the ability to recognize, analyse, and tackle complex

problems employing logical thinking, considering arguments, taking into consideration alternative solutions and taking informed choices. The critical thinker approaches problems with an analytical and systematic approach.

In embracing these concepts and the components that make up critical thinking students improve their capacity to evaluate information, analyze arguments, identify falsehoods, and make informed decisions. The skills of critical thinking are crucial to make informed decisions, solving problems and dealing with the complexity of our world.

www.ingramcontent.com/pod-product-compliance
Lightning Source LLC
Chambersburg PA
CBHW071440080526
44587CB00014B/1931